VIGNETTES FROM THE MODERN ERA

By

SCOTT FARAGHER

DEATHCAT MEDIA

COPYRIGHT 2017 Scott Faragher
ISBN: 978-0-9863726-6-7
Published By Deathcat Media, LLC
PO Box 50292
Nashville, TN. 37205
615-353-0573
Deathcatmedia.com
Email: deathcatmedia@gmail.com

Also by SCOTT FARAGHER

Music City Babylon, Inside the World of Country Music-Birch Lane, New York, 1992

The Branson, Missouri Scrapbook-Citadel, New York, 1994

The Complete Guide to Riverboat Gambling-Citadel, New York, 1995

Making it in Country Music-Citadel, New York, 1996

Nashville, Gateway to the South-Cumberland House, Nashville, 1998

New Orleans (Postcard History Series)-Arcadia, Charleston,

SC., 1999

Nashville in Vintage Postcards-Arcadia, Charleston, SC., 1999

Memphis in Vintage Postcards (With Katherine Harrington) Arcadia, Charleston, SC., 2000

Beer Signs for the Collector-Schiffer, Atglen, PA., 2001

Chattanooga, Best of the Lookout City-Milton, Chattanooga, TN., 2001

Cameras for the Collector-Schiffer, Atglen, PA., 2002

The New South (contributing author)-Insight Guides, London-2004

Porsche, the Ultimate Guide-KP Books-Iola, Wisc., 2005

The Peabody Hotel (With Katherine Harrington)-Arcadia, Charleston, SC., 2006

The Hammond Organ-Scott Faragher, Nashville, 2009

The Hammond Organ-Hal Leonard, Milwaukee, Wisc., 2011

The Arlington Resort Hotel & Spa-Scott Faragher (with Katherine Harrington)-Deathcat Media, Nashville, 2017

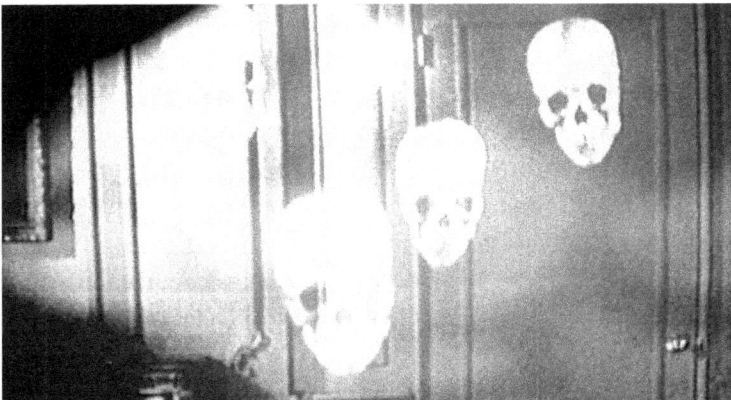

Some of these first images were from the late Imperial House in Nashville. It had been empty for years, but at one time represented the zenith of modernity. Like all of us, its ultimate fate had already been decided. There are other pictures interspersed through the text, many of which I've taken, others I just liked. There is no theme, per se, I just liked what I saw and captured it as it was at that moment. As an amateur photographer I've noticed that nothing lasts that long in the vast expanse of time.

CONTENTS

1. The Submarine
2. 14th Floor, Down Please
3. Graduation Day
4. The Cake
5. Isn't it Beautiful? Touch it!
6. El Gato
7. Fate
8. The Hubcap
9. The Wasps
10. Checkmate ! Game Over.
11. The Robbers
12. The Truth Will Set You Free
13. The American Dream
14. Time
15. The Hunt
16. The Old Man
17. The Golfer
18. Cuban Cigars
19. Veteran's Day
20. Sit Anywhere You Like
21. The Misanthrope
22. Coke to Go
23. Nigger
24. Guaranteed to Kill
25. Rush
26. She Cried
27. The Classroom Door
28. A Christmas Story
29. One Brick Too Many
30. Finally a Multimillionaire
31. I'll Show You
32. Tom
33. What Goes Around
34. Black Friday
35. Gas Station
36. On The Bridge
37. The Three Puppies
38. Attempted Murder

39. Make A Wish
40. Boss Man Ain't Gonna Like `At
41. Thanks for Giving Me a Chance
42. The Meeting
43. I Thought I Saw A Ghost
44. That Isn't Mine!
45. Express Yourself
46. The Gift of the Double Reverse Magi
47. Next !
48. The Argument
49. Smoke `em if you got `em

Hopefully you will enjoy the 'short stories' included herein. Most of them are things I experienced or that happened to persons I know, or have known. I look at these happenings in much the same way at I observe a photograph, as something fixed permanently in time, something with a definite beginning and end, one defined largely by shutter speed. And yet, everything which exists within a specific moment in time is ultimately part of a larger continuum, which hopefully survives somehow, somewhere, despite its dissolution here.

1976 Cadillac convertible. Alabama back road.

Grey Gables, Holly Springs, Mississippi

The late IMPERIAL HOUSE, Nashville

1. THE SUBMARINE

Altman looked like an Auschwitz survivor, gaunt, pale, almost skeletal in fact. He and his pal Moe Blatt, also from somewhere in New York, were friends of mine. Moe was about 6'3" tall, a tall, hulking fellow with a thick New York Yiddish accent. The three of us were in exile in the Navy at basic electronics school on base in Great Shakes, Illinois, near Chicago. I usually went with them to Jewish Services on Friday nights, at their invitation. We weren't especially interested in religious instruction of any kind. Basically, the temple put on a good feedbag after services.

One afternoon after class, I stepped into the early 1940s barracks restroom, a communal place basically unchanged from its inception in the clapboard frame two-story barracks. There were no doors on the crappers, not that it mattered to me. I was there to drain my lizard. As I entered the room, Altman was standing there next to the sink which was rapidly filling with water. In his hand, was the plastic model submarine I'd retrieved from a small round metal trashcan earlier in the day. It was just a plastic model someone had assembled, and having done so had no place to display it, so had discarded it.

The urinal was some long enamel trough about four feet in length, and affixed to the wall. It had a curious flushing cycle in that the water would rise about seven or eight inches every few minutes, and then slowly recede, sort of like the tides. Anyway, I'd thought that it would be amusing to watch the sub float with the rising water, and then ride it down every few minutes, which it was.

Altman was holding the submarine with a paper towel by the conning tower, having removed it from the urinal. I asked him why he'd removed the submarine from the pisser?

"I can't pee on a submarine," he replied quickly.

I processed his reply as quickly as he'd proffered it and concluded that he was possibly crazy, given that I'd launched the submarine into the urinal and christened it myself in the morning, so people had literally been pissing on it for hours. So what difference could it make now? On the other hand, the fact that he was in the navy might explain his reluctance to piss on it. Perhaps it was some misguided but well intentioned show of respect. This was possibly an acceptable and not completely irrational consideration, at least in theory. I was willing to accept that as a possibility in my own mind. What was however inexplicable, at least to me, was the fact that he had filled the sink with water, placed the submarine in the sink while he peed, then drained the water from the sink, took a paper towel and ceremoniously replaced the sub in the pisser, where it would once again be used for urinary target practice.

I'd watched this curious series of events without comment, but after he'd replaced the submarine I asked why he'd gone to all the trouble of filling the sink with water before he placed the sub in it.

"Oy, I toldja I can't pee on a submarine," he repeated as he left the room.

2. 14th FLOOR, DOWN PLEASE
Email: October 12

"I got a call from Padge's sister, Barbara, this morning informing me that Padge took his own life Tuesday. Padge had long suffered from depression and anxiety and talked about suicide many times, but as far as I know, he never attempted it until yesterday. Jerry and Barbara plan to have Padge's body cremated and there is no memorial service scheduled at this time. A memorial gathering may be scheduled in the weeks to come and I will keep you informed."

People always seem serious when someone dies, at least they think that perhaps they should appear serious. This is especially true when someone dies suddenly or tragically. The news was indeed sad, that someone had 'taken his own life.' That sounds better than saying that he killed himself. It somehow sounds less violent, and more like it was some type of accident as opposed to intentionally having killed oneself, which is an active premeditated act, as was the case here. There were no details other than those mentioned in the email, not at first, anyway. I called someone who I felt would likely know what had actually happened. She told me that the decedent had been depressed most all of his life, and as far as she knew had not

2

had a happy day in the last twenty years. "He'd been popular in high school," she told me, "and carried a picture of himself when he was younger, saying `he'd been handsome back then.'" He'd never been able to translate that earlier experience into his subsequent life. Hell, that was forty years ago, I thought. But what sent him over the edge literally, she said, was the reduction in free prescription drugs, the anti-depressants that he'd taken to dull his pain.

It's a terrible thing, I thought, to feel so bad that there's no other way out. I'd felt like that before, so I understood how easy it is to just slip that extra little bit. I'd been saved by the grace of God and my own eventual curiosity over what else could possibly go wrong. I mean, wasn't I at the bottom already, back then? Apparently not, but I'd held on anyway. My hell only lasted three years. His had been longer.

Padge. I liked his name, though it was one I'd never heard before or since. I hadn't seen him in fifteen years, and probably wouldn't have recognized him if I had. He'd been to my office a couple of times visiting someone I worked with back then. He'd seemed lost, as I remember, strangely disconnected, like he really wasn't fully in the moment. He struck me as someone with little internal volition, like a rudderless boat floating on the surface. I've always had little patience with people who refuse to take responsibility for their own lives. "Just get off your ass and get busy," I would've told him, if he'd asked my advice back then. "The world is full of useless, nonproductive losers. Make sure you aren't one of them." But as I've gotten older, my attitudes have changed somewhat. There are some people who just can't help themselves, for whatever reason. There is some hole they can't fill within themselves which reduces their ability to successfully function in life. Their inability to cope with the world around them is not necessarily a result of lack of opportunity, a real deficiency of intelligence, or any other specifically observable cause. It's just the way it is.

Apparently he'd held on as long as he could. One trip to the public hospital on the poor side of town, after his free prescription drug program had been cut, had proved to be more trouble than it was worth. He decided on some level that he'd actually rather die than have to regularly deal with a bunch of

3

imbeciles in order to get the medicine he needed. So, rather than go through all of that red tape again, his suicide note read, the interviews, the filling out of forms, the bus ride over, the waiting, etc. he'd rather be done with the whole business once and for all. He called 911, said that he was going to jump off the top floor of his building, and then took the elevator up, got off, and jumped.

Blood, brains, broken bones, teeth, hair, and excrement. A colorful two hundred pound meat-filled liquid water balloon dropped on the sidewalk from the fourteenth floor. Poor bastard. Poor inconsiderate bastard. Poor inconsiderate, useless bastard. How selfish, inconsiderate and narcissistic to leave a mess of that magnitude for other people to have to involuntarily witness, and somebody else to have to clean up.

Was his suicide the final desperate self-obliterating act of a sad life, an existence so fraught with pain that it could not continue even another moment? Or was it the supreme self-indulgence of one too spoiled and coddled to play the excellent hand he'd been given? One from whom nothing had been expected, and nothing rendered. "The better the excuse, the worse it is," one famous preacher had said about those who had made the decision to be unsuccessful. And what of organ donation? His life could have counted for something to somebody, somewhere, even in death, but it didn't.

With over a hundred thousand people, most of them poor, killed in an earthquake in Haiti recently, and seventy thousand known dead from an earthquake on the India-Pakistan border a couple of years ago, it's difficult to be overly sympathetic to someone who'd been born into comfortable circumstances in the land of plenty and yet had still managed to fail in spite of his many opportunities. This is especially true in light of the fact that so many, with so much less, are willing to work so hard. But then, again, he'd been someone's son, and he had two sisters. A permanent solution to a temporary problem? I don't know.

The Bhagavad Gita says to pity neither the living or the dead. Padge's lesson for me is that anybody who can't find a reason to live won't have too long to feel sorry for himself. Even the bible says that the tree which bears no fruit shall be cut down.

4

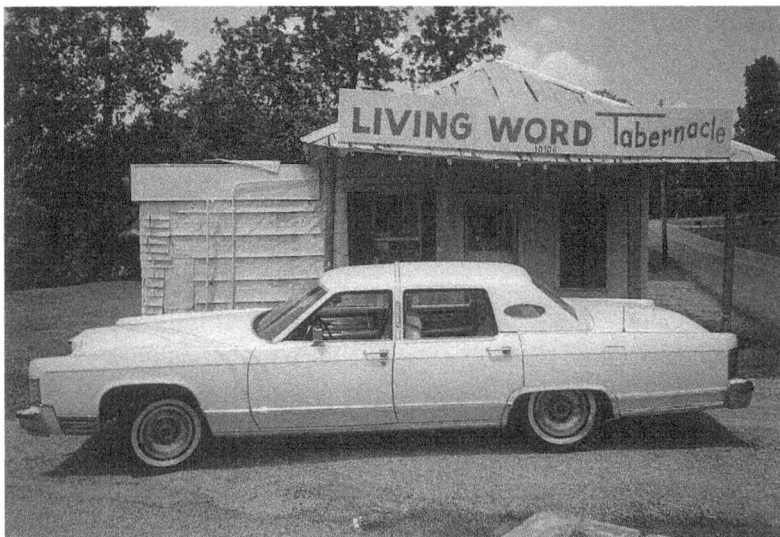

3. GRADUATION DAY

He'd arrived early, walking slowly and quietly down the deserted, highly polished hallway toward the biology lab, his classroom of nearly twenty years, on this Saturday, Graduation Day. He'd come several hours before the big event so that he could properly prepare his special surprise for the students and faculty in this rural Tennessee town without being disturbed. This had to be done just right for maximum effect. It had to be spectacular, and it would be, worthy of the nearly two decades he'd spent in this room, trying in vain, for the most part, to educate stupid hicks. Yes, they were stupid. There was no denying it, and no way of disguising the truth by calling them something else like 'slow learners', 'at risk', or 'challenged.' Their parents were stupid, their grandparents were stupid, and so were they. That was the fact of the matter. They would all be married, most within thirty days of graduation. They would all have at least three children by the age of twenty, excluding, of course the ones who were already twenty and still hadn't graduated from high school. They would, for the most part, live in trailers surrounded by low end rusting junk cars like old Ford Tauruses, and Dodge Omnis, in a yard littered with old tires and overturned rubber children's tricycles, and that redneck favorite, the trampoline. They'd smoke cigarettes, eat junk food, drink gallons of beer and Pepsi, and become fat and grotesque very early in life. And most of them would live off the taxpayer in some way or another, through programs such as food stamps and WIC which made the productive members of society, the workers, pay for their fat, and equally stupid grimy pie-faced offspring.

He looked around the room, as if seeing in his mind particular students, ones he remembered especially, for one reason or another. Yes, there was that big hulking oaf Steve, who lit cigarettes with the Bunsen burners and then bent down and smoked under the lab table, as if the teacher didn't know what he was doing, the dumb son of a bitch. He's probably pumping gas at some mini mart somewhere. Yeah, he was a brilliant student. And that's where Duwayne used to sit, the one who put the dead frog on top of the intercom speaker where it sat for days before he noticed it. And last year, Billy Bob occupied Duwayne's seat. Billy Bob had unplugged the refrigerator allowing the dissected cats to rot. Damn, that was a stinking mess. Every year it was the same shit. Each new class found it necessary to unplug the aquarium, to murder the fish, to kill and destroy everything beautiful. God damn them!

But it wasn't the students that had brought him to this point, it was a church, not any church, but it was in this town, 'the' church. In this case, the Church of Jesus The Emancipator. Over the last fifteen years its influence had spread like a cancer throughout the small town infecting its citizenry until all of the 'powers that be' in this small Tennessee town were active members of this powerful fraternity. The mayor, the police chief, the postmaster, most of the town council, the school superintendent, the fire chief, the head of the electric company, nearly everybody in any position of power was a member of the Church of Jesus The Emancipator. It was like a big spider with little webs throughout the town and the county, with the big mother spider perched atop the hill at the entrance to the town. The ACLU had no idea what was going on here. The domination and influence of this political body, and that's what it was, despite its claim of being a religious organization, had spread its tentacles throughout its dominion, altering rules and regulations and issuing decrees in accord with its collective will.

As a result of its puritanical edicts, boys and girls were not permitted to swim at the public pool at the same time. 'Mixed bathing' as it was called, had been deemed to be 'not in the public interest.' In other words, at specific times each day throughout the summer months, all boy children had to get out of the pool to let the girls in, and vice versa. The Church of Jesus The Emancipator had also decided that there need no longer be a senior prom, because dancing was not actually wholesome entertainment for teens. But then, what would you expect from a church that did not allow an organ, piano, or any other musical instrument because of some clearly twisted and misinterpreted biblical technicality?

But Bob Carter was above all, a reasonable man. Wasn't a group of people with similar interests and opinions deciding the rules for their own community the very essence of democracy? In other circumstances, perhaps. But in this town qualified people had been systematically removed from long held jobs under one phony pretext or another only to be replaced by Church of Jesus The Emancipator members, and nobody had done anything about it. Nothing had been done initially because there had been no indication that there'd been any deliberate intention to gain control and power over the lives of others. It had been done quietly and in the darkness, behind closed doors until the Church of Jesus The Emancipator had become all powerful. Now the school building contract for the new school went to a Church of Jesus The Emancipator member, and the same for the new airport expansion, and for the local street resurfacing, and on and on. And now it was too late.

And this was what had had happened to Robert Carter. Chief Smith's son had just graduated from Harry Donaldson University, the Church of Jesus The Emancipator indoctrination center and breeding ground in Memphis, with a degree in biology, and he needed a job and wanted to move back to his own home town. They couldn't just fire Carter, it would have been too obvious. Instead they added Chief Smith's son as a second biology teacher on equal footing, and then began taking classes away from Carter until there was basically nothing left, not even one biology class, the unspoken intention being to make his life so miserable that he would ultimately resign. It was clearly immoral, illegal, and just plain wrong. But that's the way it was. And now they were going to pay the ultimate price. They were all guilty, not only the evil Church of Jesus The Emancipator, but the Methodists, Baptists, and the others who'd stood by idly as their town had been stolen from them.

Carter realized that he'd been wasting time reflecting on the past and got busy, walking from burner to burner, turning the gas all the way up, each of the chrome insect-looking devices emitting a loud hiss as he turned it on. Within a matter of moments the entire biology lab sounded like a summer night. Well, then, he reflected proudly, that's it. By the time the students filed into the gym in a couple of hours, the entire school would be filled with natural gas. It would be a giant firebomb waiting for some innocent to simply pick up the phone or turn on a light switch. He looked around the biology lab, his biology lab, for the last time, and felt mixed emotions. No, not all of his students had been stupid. There was Susan Miller who in spite of her rural origins, had gone to Vanderbilt Medical School. He was proud of some of them, and this thought made the teacher smile for a moment. He was recalled to the present by the sound of a door slamming in the distance. He listened intently, standing still, trying to hear additional sounds. The hiss of the escaping gas was too loud. He would have to investigate immediately. There wasn't supposed to be anyone else here, that's why he'd come early. But nobody was going to ruin his big graduation day surprise. He'd put too much thought into it, and that's why he'd brought his pistol, some German thing his father had brought back from World War II. It was old but it worked just fine. He'd practiced last week, just in case. He hoped he wouldn't have to use it, but he would if he had to. He'd never shot anyone before, but he could. He'd rather not, but he knew he could, and he would, if he had to. Killing somebody he knew would be too personal. It's much easier to kill several hundred faceless people at a distance than to kill one person, somebody who's looking right at you, somebody you know, and who knows you. But he could if he had to.

He walked rapidly but silently in the direction of the noise.

There was nobody in sight, but somebody was here beside himself, and that would not be permitted. A light emanating from under a door indicated that it was probably Coach Wilson. The teacher opened the door, silently and quickly. Coach Wilson turned in the direction of the door, "Oh, hello Bob, what are you doing here?" he asked automatically, dismissively, then noticing the pistol, looked perplexed. Carter quickly fired three shots into the center of his chest and Coach Wilson fell immediately to the floor. Carter made certain Wilson was dead, replaced the pistol in his pocket, and calmly exited the building, got into his car and drove back home as if nothing had happened. And in his mind, nothing had happened. The ensuing inferno would incinerate several hundred evil doers and their children, as well as destroy any evidence of the shooting. The entire business would be blamed on a gas leak, an ever present possibility in the real world. He would, of course, feign shock and sadness upon hearing the news, but would never be linked to the actual event. While revenge is a dish best served cold, his would be served 'well done' in every sense of the expression.

But Carter's plan was not destined to reach fruition. Several teachers had arrived nearly simultaneously within half an hour, smelled gas, seen the door to the biology lab open, and found Coach Wilson's body. They turned off the gas, and two of them, long standing colleagues of Bob Carter, bravely drove to the biology teacher's house, told him what had happened, and took him quietly to the police station rather than forcing him to be dragged into the station handcuffed with news cameras rolling. Carter said nothing on the way to the police station, and rode quietly. There was no need to ask 'why?' They knew what had been done to Carter. The driver, English teacher Mark Harris, did ask one question of the biology teacher. "Bob, if it had been me who'd come in, instead of Coach Wilson, would you have shot me?"

"Yes" Carter, sighed without elaboration, "I probably would have."

At the trial Bob Carter did not testify in his own defense. The light had gone from his eyes. He was found guilty of murder and sentenced to life in prison. It might have been different if Bob Carter had had a life, but he hadn't. He still lived at home with his parents at age 45. Between caring for them and teaching school, there was nothing left for him in the way of a personal life. No wife, no children, no girlfriend. Despite the absence of these essentials, he'd been happy for the most part. He'd lived to teach, but even this had been taken from him.

4. THE CAKE

It was just an old, faded, three by five inch black and white photograph of a man holding a cake, nothing exceptional about the photograph, or the cake, other than he had baked it himself for his one year old daughter's first birthday. The little girl's aunt had already baked the child a birthday cake, probably out of a sense of begrudging obligation. The cake the aunt made had been poorly and hastily made, and it showed. The man didn't look especially happy either, standing there in his Sunday suit with a crooked bow tie, and why should he? His wife was dying of cancer and wouldn't live to see their daughter grow up, or the completion of the house under construction which they'd designed and intended to live in together. His wife, his other half, the love of his heart, would soon die, and his own life would become even worse, but today he couldn't foresee that. Today he'd baked his daughter a cake. She wouldn't have known the difference, one way or the other, but he would have, and that was reason enough. The first cake had been made in haste, the second was made with all the love he had to give.

This advertisement looked as if it had been made by a third grader. I doubted that anyone selling gold would have ever stopped in front of this disintegrating former gas station for that purpose. The irony in the scene was not especially subtle.

5. ISN'T IT BEAUTIFUL? TOUCH IT!

She was my first girlfriend, though she didn't know it. She was so beautiful that I nearly swooned every time I saw her. Thin, intelligent, and gorgeous. She was three years older than I was, a significant consideration at the time. But there I was, alone with her at dusk in the front seat of my grandfather's Ford. What an incredible piece of good fortune. I knew it even then. I wanted this to never end. I wanted to just stay there forever, looking into her beautiful eyes and listening to her soothing voice, but it was starting to get dark, and I knew she would have to leave soon, probably at any moment, and without notice. Anyway, she depressed the car's cigarette lighter, and out it popped a few seconds later. She removed it from its housing and showed me the glowing red business end. "Isn't it beautiful?" she asked, looking at me. "Yes," I replied, "it really is beautiful." And indeed it was, bright red and glowing. "Touch it," she said. I hesitated. "Touch it," she repeated, "it won't hurt you." I didn't know any better, after all I was only four years old, and in love. So I touched it with my finger and was burned instantly. I immediately began howling. She calmly replaced the cigarette lighter where it belonged and took off, leaving me there crying loudly. I was in great physical pain, but my emotional pain was even greater. Why had she done this ? I had trusted her. She hadn't told me that I would be burned, that it would hurt.

I tearfully told my grandfather what had happened. He laughed quietly, putting some Vaseline on the tip of my finger and then replied to my 'Why?' by saying "That's just the way girls are."

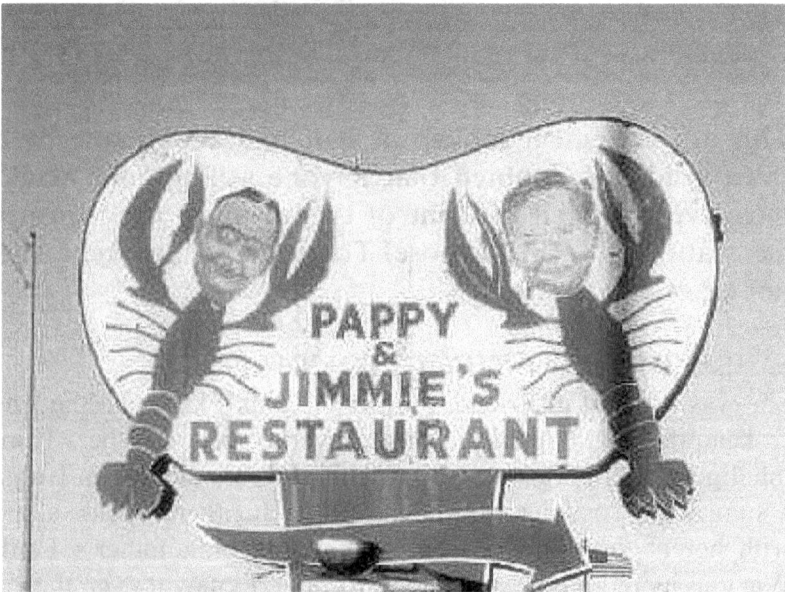

Pappy & Jimmie's, Memphis

6. EL GATO

I don't particularly like cats, well, I like them now more than I used to. I specifically remember this one cat, and one of the

English Bulldogs we had at the time. This particular bulldog was named Georgia Brown, and was the lead dog in the prancing sex-crazed group I deemed the 'Triumverate,' which consisted of female Georgia Brown, walking aimlessly around the yard or driveway, with my other dyke female bulldog Jackie atop the lead dog's hind quarters hunching furiously. The caboose was a Yorkshire terrier who joined the line, hunching with equal verve, and just as futilely as Jackie. They walked around the yard, a jumble of motion, with Georgia Brown more or less unconcerned with the two hangers on. Anyway, casual though she might have been about the incessant grinding on her hindquarters, she was extremely focused on her dislike of the cat, a furry multi-colored female drifter who'd latched on to our family when we moved into some decaying country house in the late 1960s. By the time I returned from the navy some two years later, the house had been completely restored, but the Triumverate had not changed at all, they were still at it. The hostility that Georgia Brown felt for the cat, however, had intensified in my absence and now, actively sought expression.

What generally happened was this. The bulldog would be asleep on the back porch, and the cat would carefully but pointedly get as close to the bulldog as safely possible, waving her tail in the dog's face and otherwise provoking her. When the cat got close enough that the dog thought she could catch it, the dog took off at full speed. The cat invariably jumped from the porch and quickly ducked through a hole in the stone foundation beside the air conditioning unit. The hole was just large enough for the cat to pass through, but not the bulldog, who without fail always managed to ram her head into the stone wall. I had witnessed this occurrence dozens of times with glee, always hoping that the bulldog would catch the cat. It was really something like one would see in a cartoon where there is some cat that always outsmarts a bulldog. In the cartoons, it's always a cat and a bulldog, not a cat and some other breed, and the cat always wins. This real life version always ended the same way. At length I began to think that this bulldog was just plain stupid, as they are known to be, and wondered why she kept falling for the same old trick. But the bulldog really was that stupid, and the cat was that provocative, and also that fast.

One afternoon, however the bulldog almost got her revenge. In the front yard, the cat had climbed a maple tree and was attempting to get a bird's nest. But the cat had gotten far higher than it intended to, and was now being dive bombed by frantic birds who were driving it ever closer to the thinning end of a long branch. I'd been alerted to the proceedings by the loud barking of my bulldog who was waiting on the ground for the inevitable. The bulldog would alternately sit nervously or jump up and down against the tree trunk, slinging saliva in Pavlovian expectation, waiting for the cat to fall. As much as I disliked the cat, and felt that the bulldog deserved some type of reparations for all of the times she'd been intentionally harassed while minding her own business, I knew that this would have meant a horrible, bloody, bone crunching death for the cat. I reluctantly took the dog back into the house until the birds did drive the cat off the end of the branch and it fell to the ground, apparently none the worse for the experience.

For a few days, all was well. The cat recovered from the discomfort of a fifteen foot fall, and the bulldog slept on the back porch, as usual, with one eye open, and her cheeks spread out on the floor. But it wasn't long before the cat was again harassing the sleeping dog, having soon forgotten that it would have been devoured but for my kind intercession. Now, it seemed that the bulldog had finally learned to tolerate the cat's provocation. She must have realized that the cat was simply too fast, and that crashing head first into the stone wall, yet again, was pointless. The cat continued, getting ever closer to the sleeping bulldog, waving its tail provocatively, but without any response. The bulldog simply ignored the cat, and slept motionlessly. But the bulldog's eye, that is, its one open eye had been watching, moving around like a searchlight, factoring distance, speed, in short, estimating if the cat could be caught perhaps this time. The cat, over the next few days moved ever closer to the sleeping bulldog, again eliciting no response, and I decided that the bulldog had indeed finally realized that it would never be able to catch the cat under the existing circumstances, ever. But then one day I opened the back door as the cat was in the process of waving its tail in the sleeping bulldog's face. The sound of the opening door startled the cat, who looked up for just an instant. As it did so, the bulldog snapped off the end of the cat's tail with one clean, lightning fast motion. It was really that fast. Again, the cat jumped off the porch and ran under the house, only this time, howling like you never heard, with the bulldog in hot pursuit, once more smashing its head into the stone wall. This time, however, the bulldog had had the last laugh, and at least three inches of the cat's tail. All sorts of things come to mind as I think about this event. From the bulldog's perspective, "Good things come to those who wait", "The race isn't to the swift but to the strong", "All things in time" and so on. I never again saw the cat intentionally provoke the bulldog. Apparently it had at last grasped the wisdom of the injunction, "Let sleeping dogs lie."

The car was big, but the boulder was bigger.

7. FATE

One night many years ago, I sat down in front of the television just in time for the 10:00 local news. A man was killed, it reported, in a freak accident when lightning struck the cliffs high above the highway and dislodged a large boulder which landed upon his car as he passed beneath them. I immediately recognized that location as being on the old highway from Nashville to Chattanooga, between Murfreesboro and Manchester, basically in the middle of nowhere. I'd driven that stretch of road many times. The images of his damaged car were shown along with the story. The car was just like mine, a late 1970s Lincoln Town Car, one of the largest passenger cars ever made. It was in good condition overall, except for the section of roof beneath which the driver had been sitting. That section had been completely crushed by the giant boulder.

Until the very moment he died, the driver had probably felt himself to be invincible in that car, given its massive size and weight. I felt the same way when I drove mine. After all, one of these same giant Lincolns had been intentionally placed on the railroad track in front of a speeding freight train by this very television station several months earlier, to sensationally depict the 'Dangers of Railroad Crossings.' When the freight train had hit this giant Lincoln broadside at around 40 miles an hour, it didn't drag the car down the railroad track as expected, or shred it into an unrecognizable mass of twisted steel. The train had merely knocked the car off of the tracks and kept moving. Having witnessed this event on television and seen the minimal structural damage to the car, I considered myself to be in the safest car on the highway.

Literally millions of cars had passed beneath that same bluff without incident on that eighty year old stretch of two lane road. It had been the main highway to Florida before the Interstate had been built nearby, and yet this one time, lightning had somehow struck the bluff just a fraction of a second before the car arrived beneath it, giving the giant boulder just enough time to fall and land on the car's roof, directly above the driver's seat, where the man was sitting. It could have landed on either side of his car, or in front of, or behind his car after it passed, or even upon the trunk, or the hood, or any other part of the roof, and the man would probably not even have been injured, but it hadn't. It had landed, as if precisely and purposefully aimed, guided by some unseen agency to fall specifically upon the only part of the car where it could have, and did in fact, instantly kill the driver.

I continued to feel as safe in this old car of mine as I ever had. The chances of such a thing occurring again, especially to me, were infinitely impossible, and yet I'm sure the man who'd experienced this event would have said the same thing, that is, until it actually happened to him. Most people would probably consider the event to have been random bad luck, or `just one of those things,' but I've thought about it a lot, and to me, it seems like a cosmic hit. The whole thing was just too well orchestrated and precisely executed to have been merely an accident. This man was intentionally singled out and killed, or `called home,' if you prefer the phrase. For whatever reason or reasons, his time was up. When God calls, we will answer the phone, and that's that.

Someone wiser than myself, once observed that it sometimes seems as if our lives are like that of a dog running on a chain attached to a clothesline in the back yard, and nothing more. Some of the clotheslines are longer than others, as are the chains attached to them. Like the dog, we run as far and as fast as we want, having the illusion of freedom. Since we don't know how long our particular `cosmic clothesline' is, or the length of the chain attached from it to our neck, we always get snapped back, and often hard, depending on our speed when we reach the end of our particular chain. Then we quickly discover that our freedom is illusory after all, and that our fate, is ultimately not in our own hands.

17

8. THE HUBCAP

In my own defense, I can't say with absolute certainty that it was actually 'his' hubcap in the first place, although his 1970 Cadillac convertible was missing a hubcap identical to this one, and we both lived nearby. I was driving down Harding Road and saw it lying there off to the side of the road across the street from Belle Meade Mansion. I recognized it as belonging to a 1970 Cadillac convertible, like the one I was driving. I turned around pulled over to the side of the road, and picked it up.

I saw him a few days later and said, "It looks like you're missing a hubcap."

"I don't know where the son of a bitch is," he replied.

"Well, I happen to have an extra one which I'd sell you for $25." He agreed to my price, so I reached into the trunk, withdrew the hubcap, and he paid me for it. If he'd bitched about my price or anything else, I'd have probably just given it to him since it was most likely his anyway and had probably rolled off while he was driving down the street. But it was just much more fun this way, for me at least. I honestly don't know whether it was the same hubcap as he'd lost, but it probably was. I took the $25 and bought an entire set of 1969 Cadillac hubcaps, which I liked better, anyway.

These people at the veterinarian's office were dressed for Halloween and I liked this picture.

9. THE WASPS

It was just one wasp in a small nest above my front door. I don't generally mind wasps as they aren't especially aggressive, and are an essential part of summer, here but for a brief time. Of course, I've been stung by wasps before, but usually by accident, when I wandered too close to their home territory. One wasp in a small nest on the outside of my front door was no big deal. As the summer progressed, however, the nest grew larger and there were more wasps. It was so gradual that I didn't really notice at first. After all they were under the bottom of my front porch, some distance above the front door. What difference did it make? Soon, however, there were many wasps and the nest had grown exponentially, and now there were wasps always flying around the yard, and around me when I opened my front door. They posed no problem, at first. They minded their business and I minded mine. Generally, whenever I opened my door, I'd see them perched on the outside of their nest, up there, looking down at me with their beady insect eyes. One day, however, seemingly overnight, they began buzzing close to me in a decidedly hostile and threatening manner, despite the fact that I had most generously allowed them to build their nest in my space. At first, their buzzing was merely annoying. Finally, one morning, without provocation, several of them suddenly stung me simultaneously and unexpectedly. I cursed them and hurried inside.

I left immediately through my back door, drove straight to the hardware store and bought a large spray can of wasp and hornet killer. When it turned dark and the wasps had returned to their nest above my front door, I again casually walked through my front door, now armed with my large, brightly colored can of insecticide. Holding the can aloft at arm's length, I precisely aimed the nozzle in the direction of the nest. One brief burst of the toxic spray did the job instantly. I was amazed by the efficiency of the insecticide. All of the wasps were dead so quickly that they were literally frozen in place. They literally didn't have enough time to even move, let alone, to attack me. It was really that fast. Their motionless bodies, frozen both in space and time sort of reminded me of the people who died at Pompeii. I casually retrieved a broom stick, knocked the nest to the floor, stomped it, ground it into the bricks under foot, and then casually kicked it over the side of the porch into the bushes. So much for my open door philosophy of live and let live. The truth is that there is no such thing as live and let live. Each species and each group, whether man or insect, strives for domination. Their wasp culture and my own were incompatible. When through ignorance, or mistaken altruistic feelings you fail to acknowledge that which you've empirically observed, it is always to your own detriment.

10. CHECKMATE ! GAME OVER

I didn't know Mike that well, at least not at first. He was a long standing friend of my new girlfriend. I wasn't threatened by his presence because he had been dumped by his true love Nancy while he'd been away at college, in North Dakota, and was still suffering, several years after the fact. In Mike's absence, Nancy had been wooed and wowed by some slick, fast talker who'd put on a good act, one for which she'd fallen. She wanted the good life and she wanted it right away. Steve could provide that…now. She was tired of waiting on Mike, who was still in college, notwithstanding the fact that he'd worked throughout high school, and over the summers, and was paying his own way. She wanted the world and she wanted it now. She moved in with the other man while her boyfriend was away at school, not bothering to mention her new arrangement. She simply stopped corresponding with him, wouldn't answer his letters, wouldn't talk to him on the phone, and wouldn't see him. In desperation, Mike rode down to Kentucky in the winter on his motorcycle, to find her, to try and understand what was happening, and why. He was genuinely worried about her. He hit a deer in the cold darkness, on the way down, causing him to end up on the street and on the ice. He literally almost froze to death. This was of no consequence to her. She still wouldn't see him, and wouldn't take his phone calls. And, of course, Nancy's friends covered for her, not telling Mike the truth, that Nancy had moved in with another man. Finally, Mike's best friend decided to put him out of his misery, since nobody else would, and told him the sad truth, ironically, on his birthday.

Finally, faced with the painful reality of his situation, that his best had not been good enough, he went on with his life, despite having had his heart broken. Like most men in his situation, he reasoned that the fastest way to get over any woman is to place as many women as possible between himself and the one who broke his heart, as quickly as possible. Within a fairly short period after realizing that he'd been betrayed, he ended up in bed with another girl. This one was recently divorced herself, and already had a `pup' as he referred to women with children from a previous relationship. Well, they hit it off, that is, neither found the other to be totally repugnant, and she turned up pregnant. Since he'd been done wrong so recently, he decided to take the high ground and so he suggested that, given the circumstances, they should get married. They made wedding arrangements immediately, and as soon as these had been finalized, she realized that she hadn't been pregnant after all. Imagine that. Being the gentleman that he was, he married her anyway, despite the fact that he was still pining away for his lost love. After all, the wedding arrangements had already been made. It was too late to turn back now. In very short order, she was pregnant again, this time, in fact, and bore him a beautiful son. Now, he was truly trapped, a stranger in a strange land. Her family lived there, her parents, her sister. Her `pup' was in school there in North Dakota, far away from his home, up in the frozen wasteland, a mere stone's throw from the Canadian border. Now his original intention of finishing school and returning home to teach in the small country town of his birth would never be realized. He was stuck there forever, in this frozen place which he hated, far away from family and friends.

Meanwhile at home in Kentucky, his lost love had split with her boyfriend, after the passage of eleven years, and was again available, and wiser. The boyfriend, the one who would give her everything she thought she wanted, hadn't turned out as nice as she had imagined him to be. Over time, he'd mistreated her and, during the dissolution of their long standing relationship, shamelessly attempted to deprive her of all their jointly owned property. Now she was sorry for what had happened, the way she had treated Mike, the one who'd really loved her, and that she'd been unwilling to wait for the material things she'd thought she'd always wanted so much.

She'd cruelly thrown him away for someone of no substance, and for what? The supreme irony was that the big talker dumped her on her birthday, a coincidence not lost on her. As they say, he'd truly taken the best years of her life. Now, another fifteen years has passed. Nancy still lives by herself, and does not date. Mike, on the other hand, is still stuck in the frozen wasteland, but has adapted and survived, and if not happy, seems content, though sometimes, in private moments, he is haunted by what his life might have been.

11. THE ROBBERS

When I was in my teens I was frequently told by my mother that not only did I lack judgme nt but that everybody my age lacked judgment. It was an affliction that remained unchanged even as I got older. She frequently, and totally without provocation, cited numerous examples so that I would not forget that I didn't have much sense. When I was about fourteen, she told me about the son of a friend of hers. "Now that boy exercised good judgment," she said, and proceeded to tell me the story. Apparently the young lad, who had just recently got his driver's license, was out on a date in the family car one night when it began to rain. Supposedly the windshield wipers wouldn't work. "Do you know what he did?" she asked. I really didn't care one way or the other but I knew that I was going to get the answer anyway, so I said "No, what?"

"Instead of trying to drive home and risk possibly having an accident, he called his parents, and they came and got him. Now that's an example of good judgment."

Several examples of my own lack of judgment come to mind now, like when I traded my grandfather's Colt .45 six gun, "the gun that killed Sitting Bull" for something, to a friend, or the time that I took the family car (I had no driver's license) while my parents were in Mexico, and ran into the back of Mrs. Wilson's new yellow Thunderbird convertible, or the time when my parents went out for the evening and returned home unexpectedly early to find beer dripping from the ceiling and articles of girls' clothing scattered about the house. But the most notorious local example of adolescent lack of judgment came from my friend John Hitt, who lived one street over, on Esteswood. His actions superseded anything I ever did or could've even imagined.

One Friday evening his parents went out with some friends for dinner. This, John reasoned, would be an opportune time to take the other family car for a spin, not a road trip, but just a pleasant drive to nearby Green Hills. So John and several of his friends, all well known to me, started the car, a 1962 Corvair sedan, and off they went. Not being a particularly good driver, John immediately somehow managed to dent the car. He panicked knowing he would really be in serious trouble, not merely for damaging the car, but for taking it out in the first place when he was only fourteen years old. The adolescents pooled their considerable intellectual powers and quickly arrived at an ingenious solution, one which would absolutely solve the problem on all levels. If John hadn't taken the car, it follows that he couldn't have wrecked it, and therefore would not 'be in trouble.' His syllogistic logic was correct, although his initial premise was flawed. The conspirators returned to John's house, broke the glass on the back door window, knocked over and stomped some furniture, kicked in the television screen, and generally trashed the entire house, taking a few more or less valuable items, thus providing verifiable evidence that a thief or thieves had indeed broken into the house while John was over at a friend's. The most important part of their well considered plan consisted of driving the slightly damaged car the two miles to nearby Percy Warner Park where they would push it down the steep hill from the Belle Meade Blvd. overlook, with its hundred or so descending stone steps. They would then simply walk back to John's friend's house. John could casually saunter home later, after his parents had returned from dinner, and be shocked, amazed, and most importantly, horrified, that such a thing could've happened in this quiet residential neighborhood.

The police were immediately called to the scene by John's parents upon their return, and quickly determined that it was probably an inside job. Since John had been there when his parents left for dinner, the police speculated that it was likely that he was in some way involved. Less than five minutes after his arrival, and without the necessity of a spotlight, a rubber hose, or tobacco deprivation, John tearfully confessed. Needless to say, he was grounded. When this story made the rounds at the local bridge club, it served as an example of the overall 'general lack of judgment' of all members of my age group, and for years was recalled by all neighborhood parents as a valid reason why their children were not permitted to do certain things. I invariably protested that I would never get caught doing anything that stupid, not that I wouldn't do it, but that I wouldn't get caught. At the time of the incident, many of us were angered that John had given the neighborhood parents so much power through his carelessness. Even now, many years later as I remember the incident I involuntarily exclaim, "What a dumb ass!"

12. THE TRUTH WILL SET YOU FREE

"If you are truly sorry for what you have done, then you must confess your sin in front of the church," the betrayed wife insisted.

"I'll do anything you ask, whatever you want, but I'm so ashamed of what I've done, that I think it would only serve to embarrass you. And that would hurt you even more than I have already. Nobody knows about the situation but the three of us, at least as it stands now. If I confess it in front of the entire congregation then everyone who matters to us, to you, will know about it, all of our friends. They'll view us differently, from that moment forward. Understand me, I'm willing to do anything you ask. You want her fired, she's gone. It's done. You want a new car, it's yours. Whatever you want. I would even do that, confess in church, if I thought that would help matters, but I think that it would only hurt you. It would hurt me too, but I think it would hurt you more."

"But I haven't done anything," she protested angrily, "I didn't violate our marriage vows. I didn't disgrace my spouse, or bring shame on our family. I wasn't grinding away on some stranger, hiding it from you. You did that. You're in the wrong, not me. I won't be disgraced, you will."

"But darling…"

"Don't you dare call me darling, not after what you've done. I already have a new car. It's three years old, but it's new enough. You can't buy me off. That's an even bigger insult than your infidelity. Do you really think that I'm so shallow that

I'd be satisfied with some shiny trinkets? You've broken my heart, and I'm hurt, hurt and angry. You've hurt me, but now you are making me even angrier. No, I think it would probably be better all the way around if you just left now, and check into a hotel room somewhere until I decide what I want to do. I don't think I want you in the house anymore, not after what you've done. I mean it. Don't make me call the police."

Call the police? Is she out of her mind? I paid for this house. Hell, I'm still paying for it. I'm not about to leave. She can leave if she wants to, but not me. She's not going to be able to charge in a courtroom that I abandoned her. No way. "OK, you win, I'll sleep at the office for a day or so, and then come back."

"No, you won't," she called after him angrily, "I'll call you if and when I want you to come back, but I can't say if or when that will be. But I can tell you this. If I call your office and find out that slut Tammy is still there, you won't ever be coming back, I'll see you in court. I mean it."

And she did mean it. Jesus, he couldn't believe that he'd been found out. If that bitch Tammy hadn't called the house. He'd told her not to call the house…ever. How many times had he told her not to call the house? Hell, she probably did it on purpose, to push matters between them. He was sorry, sorry for being caught. Lipstick on one's collar is bad enough, but lipstick on one's underpants can't be explained. He'd had to confess, she'd cornered him, blindsided him unexpectedly. He had no valid excuse. She'd probably hired a private detective to follow him around. Who knows for how long? She was that enterprising, and that devious. Well, it would all blow over in a couple of days, or weeks. She'll forget about it sooner or later. In the meantime, he'd better tread the straight and narrow. Work, lunch, the gym, and home, that is, if he got to go home, to his own house, just in case he was being tailed. To make matters worse, there was no way of knowing how much his wife already knew, and how much was mere speculation. She might have been bluffing, but it was too late now, he'd sung like a canary when she confronted him. He always started to laugh at inappropriate times, like when he was getting ready to lie. And she knew it too, she always knew. Jesus, why did he do that? Damn! He'd have looked guilty even if he hadn't been.

After three weeks Bob was tired of the office, and while his boss was understanding and patient, he had to find somewhere else to live or he would likely lose his job. He had to move somewhere else now, without forcing his boss to evict him. Personal problems were not why he'd been hired. And Tammy? He didn't have the authority to fire her, and if he did, what justification could there be? He was every bit as guilty as she was. If she ought to be fired, than he should also be fired. Hopefully nobody at the office knew anything about it, but he couldn't be sure.

His wife hadn't called, at least that he knew of, and the longer his exile lasted, the more likely she was to be able to get along without him, and he knew what that could mean. He had to get back in her good graces at any cost, whatever it took. "By any means necessary," as Malcolm X had said. But she wouldn't take his calls, and he'd left dozens of messages. Now her phone wouldn't even receive messages, she'd turned off her answering machine. This had to end, the sooner the better, but how?

On the advice of a friend, he'd seen a lawyer. The attorney's words had not been particularly comforting. "You are in a decidedly tenuous position," he'd said. "She has the ball, so to speak, and the stadium, and the referees. You have two options, as I see it, neither of which are desirable, but we'll get to those in a minute. You say that she hasn't called you for money. That could be either bad or good. It depends. I'm glad that you are continuing to make regular deposits into her checking account. That will show good faith on your part, however this ends. You've also told me that there have been no unusual charge account or credit card purchases. That's good for you, from a financial standpoint. On the other hand, if she were planning to divorce you, her lawyer, any lawyer, would most likely advise her against doing anything which would make her look greedy, or vengeful. She's the victim here, and her power in this situation stems from that position. I advise you not to change anything financially right now, that is, if you want her to take you back, which is what you have expressed to me. If you were to close any credit card or charge accounts, such an action would likely be construed as hostile, if not by herself, then certainly by her legal counsel. And under no circumstances, I repeat, no circumstances should you ever mention, or even imply that you've seen or ever even considered seeing an attorney. I mean never, not even ten years hence, unless, of course, she files for a divorce. That would be a different matter."

"Do you think she has a lawyer?" Bob asked, stunned by the thought.

"Most certainly. That probably happened within the first few days. She's the one holding the cards, all of the cards. That you haven't heard from her attorney after a month or so most likely means that she's still thinking about it, that she hasn't decided whether to take you back or not. So, as I was saying, if you want her back, you do not want to do anything which could tip the balance out of your favor. Don't do anything further to irritate her."

"What should I do in the interim?"

"You know her better than anyone else," the lawyer said. "You know the best way to win her back, and basically that's what you're going to have to do. She has time, energy, and emotion invested in you and your children. That is a factor which is likely, well, it could be in your favor. But women today have an inner sense of independence that they didn't possess forty years ago, or at least were less likely to express. She might be only too happy to use this opportunity to start a new life at your expense. In my job, I've seen it all."

"She has a kind heart, that's the real reason I married her. Now that I've had some time on my own, I realized that I was happy the way things were. I should never have cheated on her. I never meant to. It was just one of those things. I don't know. If I could undo what I've done, I certainly would."

"I've discovered that one of the essential components of that ever illusive `happiness' everyone talks about, is its simple recognition. Many people are happy but never stop to think about it, and therefore don't realize it, until after the fact, until after they've undermined it by their own actions. It is a common mistake, on both sides of the fence," the attorney said.

"You said that I had two options," the husband said.

"Actually, given your desires in the matter," the attorney

advised, "you have only one. Just wait and see what she does. In the meantime you should do whatever you can to placate her, and you should do whatever she demands, short of killing yourself. You have broken her trust, and have rent the bond which joined you together. Some sort of heavy penance is required, and will be exacted. You can count on that. Moreover, it must be accepted gracefully, willingly, and without protest. Hopefully, she will take you back and you won't require my services beyond today. If she does reconsider in your favor, you need to remember this day, the past month or so, and what you've been through as a result of your carelessness. It's easy to get sidetracked by some hot babe at work, or anywhere else. Finding someone who will put up with you on a day to day basis, for years, even after she finds out who you really are, is of much greater value than a figurative roll in the hay with some appealing stranger. You've made the mistake of confusing rampant emotions for love, but I see the same thing almost every day. I hope this works out for you, and I hope that you've learned your lesson. Believe me, divorce is an expensive and destructive process, something to be avoided under most circumstances, especially in your case, where there are children and substantial assets involved."

Bob took the attorney's advice and went about his day to day business, but additionally began a letter writing campaign to his estranged wife, recalling the many happy times they'd shared together, and how they had struggled in the early years of their marriage. He'd sent her flowers every day for over a week, hoping to persuade her to take him back.

Finally, after nearly six weeks, she'd reached him by phone one Friday night at his hotel room and agreed to take him back. He would be permitted to move back to the house which he was paying for, his children would again be allowed to speak with him, and they would `see how things progressed.' He would not be treated as he had before, at least not initially. That would take time, she told him, a long time. Her trust in him had been seriously compromised. But in light of all they'd been through together, and her sense that his contrition was genuine, and with the persuasion of their children, he could return home next week. There was, however, one absolute condition upon which this all hinged. He must openly and fully confess his sin before the congregation at their church, this Sunday, as was the custom. This would in no way repair the damage that had been done, but it would satisfy her sense of justice. His confession would somehow, she reasoned, allow them a starting point from which to again begin their journey together. Bob accepted her proposal immediately. He was only too willing to take this extreme step despite the shame it would bring upon him. It would be embarrassing, and it wouldn't be easy, but he was truly contrite. If this was what she required, then so be it. He would follow his attorney's advice. He knew that she'd give him the silent treatment, and the cold shoulder for a while, but at least he'd be back home.

When Sunday came, Bob arrived at church at 10:45, and found a seat at the front of the sanctuary where the distance to the minister's podium would be as short as possible. He sweated blood through the ceremony, awaiting that part of the service where sins were confessed to all present. At the appointed time, he sat there in silence as three other penitent parishioners preceded him, largely unaware of what they'd even said. He raised his hand, the minister called his name, and he stepped to the front of the church, without looking back, until he turned to face the congregation. He stood there in silence for a moment, scanning the crowd for his wife's face, which he eventually found. As he spoke, haltingly, he looked directly at her, addressing her, for the moment unaware of anyone else in the room. He spoke from the heart, tearfully and truthfully confessing his unfaithfulness. Her face was in her hands as he spoke, and he could see that she was crying. He'd truly hurt her deeply, but he'd hurt himself as well, much more than he'd ever suspected, even after he'd had a miserable six weeks to think about it.

The congregation was visibly moved by his contrite, heartfelt confession, the first requisite step toward forgiveness, a step which he'd taken, even if timidly at first. At the conclusion of his profession of guilt, his wife rose from her seat, turned, and exited the rear door of the church. Bob then joined two of the elders in a prayer, after which the minister spoke a few words to the congregation, and then told Bob, "You'd better go to your wife now." As Bob followed, he was greeted outside the sanctuary door by a well-dressed young man who handed him a piece of paper, some church bulletin or other, Bob imagined, stuffing it in his pocket without even looking at it. By the time he retrieved his overcoat from the cloak room and reached the church parking lot, his wife was gone.

"Thank you, Jesus," He shouted under his breath, thrilled once more to be alive. As they say, confession is good for the soul. He felt like a new man. He would now, as Jesus had directed, 'go and sin no more.'

He immediately drove to his residence expecting to find his wife and children waiting in joyous celebration for his return. What he found instead was that the locks to the house had been changed, and that two security guards had been hired to prevent him from entering his own home. Only then did he read the paper he'd casually stuffed into his pocket, a court summons. He lost everything in the subsequent divorce that followed. He continued to pay for the house and its maintenance, his children's private schooling, medical insurance for them as well as his ex-wife, child support, and even alimony. After all, hadn't she sacrificed her own career to be a homemaker for them? His lawyer had not contested the terms of the divorce. After all, the errant husband had confessed his sin in public, a sincere speech that had been recorded by his wife's lawyer, an acceptable and legal practice under the laws of the state in which they resided.

The lesson here is that no woman should be underestimated, ever. No matter how well you might think you know one, you will never completely know her. The lawyer had been right. Finding a woman who is willing to put up with you for years, even after she's discovered who you really are, is truly the pearl of great price, and above all, she should not be crossed.

13. THE AMERICAN DREAM

I saw her at the Starbucks last year, the Chinese woman who, along with her husband, had once operated Peking Garden, Nashville's first real Chinese restaurant. I'm sure that seemed to have been in another lifetime for her, though it had been just twenty years ago. She was expensively dressed, and looked nice, standing there alone, waiting on her coffee. I doubted that she would remember me after all of this time, but I remembered her. What I remembered about her was that the restaurant had been so nice. I've never been to China but this woman and her husband had gone to great pains to create a unique dining experience for all of the restaurant's many patrons. It was decorated with ornate rosewood lanterns, exotic wood carvings and bamboo. The building itself had been located on Division Street, right on the edge of Nashville's thriving music business community, and had earlier been a Pizza joint named Melfi's.

Since I worked close by, and the food was excellent, I ate there frequently. There is a certain 'holiness' for lack of a better word, inherent in anything done well and done lovingly. This was obvious for anyone to see who cared to look at Peking Garden, and while I ate there often, I was always aware that this was a special place. I was known on sight by the two owners, the man and his wife, the woman I now beheld across the room. I never knew their names, and they never knew mine, but I was always greeted with a smile. What I noticed especially back then, was that they were always there, both of them, morning, noon, and night, that they were well dressed, drove nice cars, and were prosperous. The American dream had worked well for them, and they had worked hard to make that happen.

As I looked at the Chinese woman standing there by herself, I decided that I should speak to her. I approached her, introduced myself, and told her how much we had enjoyed her restaurant, that all of us, everybody in the music business had loved it. "You were the first real Chinese restaurant in Nashville," I said, "and the best. Your dinner menu was extensive and everything was so wonderful." She had not recognized me at first, and perhaps still didn't, but the mention of her restaurant immediately caused her eyes to light. She was happy to talk about the restaurant, and agreed with me that it was the first and still had not been surpassed. When I mentioned her husband, and how sorry I was for what had had happened to him, she instantly lowered her eyes. It was obviously still a source of great pain for her. I again spoke of her restaurant and how much it had meant to all of us and how we still remembered it. I told her good bye and that I hoped she was doing well. She thanked me for remembering her and taking the time to speak.

The restaurant had done extremely well during its heyday. The owners had bought an expensive and elegant, though not ostentatious house in the city's prosperous Forest Hills area, a house which I passed unknowingly everyday as I drove to my office. But then one day as I picked up the morning paper, I'd read how her husband had been awakened in his sleep the night before, and murdered by some robber, some useless, good for nothing piece of crap who'd probably never done an honest day's work in his stupid, pointless life.

The police caught the stupid bastard, they always do, sooner or later, this time sooner. The perpetrator in this case was some disheveled young white man in his late twenties, some God Damned hick, some stupid, useless, hick. He was duly tried, convicted, and imprisoned for life, which in Tennessee, means that, let's see, it's been more than twenty years. He's probably been out of the slammer for at least ten years, and is now going on with his life as if nothing had ever happened.

But something had happened. This moron's feeble attempt at robbery had taken another person's life. It was not his to take, but he had done so anyway. Not only had he taken the man's life, he'd taken the life of the man's wife, and he had taken their lives together. She'd tried to hold on, to keep the business open, but her husband's murder had cast a pall on the place, and she closed Peking Garden for good soon thereafter. The restaurant building was empty for years, housed several other unsuccessful businesses, and then was eventually torn down. I still pass the their former home frequently and see it perched up on the hill, a beautiful house, still, but now haunted by the sorrowful and cruel act that happened there one night. I sometimes think how I would have dealt with the intruder, how my dogs would have literally torn him to pieces, or how I would have taken his head off with a shotgun blast, but it had not happened to me, it had happened to some nice, hard-working man in his own house, minding his own business.

14. TIME

I received a call from my mother asking me if I wanted to come over for lunch at the old folks home with her and Dad. Old people make me uncomfortable, but I'd been working on one thing or another around the house and could use a break, so I accepted the invitation and told her I'd be over in about twenty minutes, and meet her downstairs. The place is nice, clean, and open, with well-dressed affluent, although aged residents. I don't relate well to people in groups, and old people in groups are equally disconcerting. I walked through the front doors past the front desk, down the hall and into the dining room. As I scanned the sea of white hair I saw my parents at a table for four and joined them there. Their friends passed by the table exchanging greetings with my parents. I dreaded each visitor. Old people make me uncomfortable. Then there was also the possibility that my mother would invite someone to join us. This likely probability made me even more uncomfortable. I came to visit my parents, not a bunch of people I don't know.

"Hello, Judge Swiggart," my mother said as another group of three senior citizens passed.

"Judge Swiggart was a Dauntless pilot in the Pacific," my father observed.

The Douglas Dauntless was a small torpedo bomber with a pilot and one gunner which was based on aircraft carriers. It was sort of a sports car, as far as navy planes were concerned, much smaller, faster, and lighter that the Grumman Avenger, another carrier based torpedo bomber. I knew that much.

"Hello, Judge Swiggart," I said, "I went to school with your son, Jimmy, at BGA. How's he doing?"

"Well," the judge replied with a smile, "at least he says he's doing alright." The judge and his party moved on and another couple came by, long time friends of my mother, Ethel Lee, and her husband.

"William was a B-24 pilot," my father observed. He was shot down over Germany, was captured, and escaped."

"Thanks for your service," I said, "you guys were the toughest." And they were. Anytime I'm around people of that era I'm truly amazed. My own father, a tank commander, Pepper Bruce, a P-40 pilot, Tavy Doty a B-17 pilot, Sam Butts, shooting deck guns at kamikazes. I'd grown up around these people, friends of my parents. But one thing I'd noticed about all of the World War II veterans I'd known is that they generally didn't talk much about it. They'd done what they had to do, made it back, and that was that. The B-24 pilot and his wife exchanged greetings and moved on. I was somewhat disappointed. I would have loved to have heard his adventures.

Another woman approached the table and my mother invited her to join us. "Jesus," I thought. The woman sat down, and I stood up, and then sat down again. "I can't stay," she said, "but I'll visit a moment." She mentioned to my mother that she really didn't understand some book my mother had lent her, and that she was going to return it. In her hands was a framed photo, I surmised, probably an 8'x 10'judging from its size. I could only see its back, so I didn't know what it was. My mother asked her what she had. That's one thing I've noticed about old people, they have no hesitation in asking questions, often personal questions of others they often don't even know. In this case, they were friends, or at least acquaintances. The woman held up the frame, its face toward us, and I saw three military medals against a dark velvet background. One was a Purple Heart, another was a Silver Star, and the third I didn't recognize. "These were my husband's" she said, "I was showing them to someone down the hall."

I recognized the Purple Heart, because my father had received two of them in World War II. I knew the Silver Star was for valor. "They're beautiful," I said, "they look brand new," and they did.

"No," she said, "they were sent to me when my husband was killed in action in 1945. We'd only been married a year and a half before he was killed."

I didn't know what to say. What could I say to someone who had suffered such a loss at such a young age, and managed to survive? I was ashamed for having not wanted her to join us. I subsequently learned that she had eventually remarried, and had three children with her second husband, who'd recently died.

Every person in that room, every white haired, frail, hobbling man or woman had a story. They'd all laughed, had hopes and dreams, victories and disappointments, had loved, and lost, and had endured.

What amazed me, even more than the B-24 pilot who'd been shot down, was this woman who'd lost her first husband, the war hero, and had never forgotten him, even after all of these years, despite the fact that she'd remarried and had three children, and had recently lost her second husband of more than fifty years. She'd always carried her first husband's memory in her heart, and still did, more than sixty years after he was killed. The suffering that we, as humans endure, and, for the most part survive, is beyond understanding. I'd always, as a matter of course, been told to 'respect my elders,' and did so as a matter of courtesy, without much thought as to why. Now I know why. Anyone who has survived to the age of eighty is deserving of respect, if for no other reason than sheer tenacity. I felt ashamed that I'd been so unwilling to share a few minutes of my time with someone I didn't know, and didn't want to know, someone who, as it turned out, taught me so much in such a short time.

15. THE HUNT

I learned about killing early. When I was eight years old, my next door neighbor got a BB gun for Christmas. Between his cat and BB gun, the bird population at my end of the street was decimated. I envied him, not that he killed helpless birds, but that he had a gun. I wanted to shoot like the cowboys or detectives on TV. I wanted to shoot something, anything. So, after several months of my constant harassment my friend took me shooting, hunting rather. He gave me tips on gun safety, showed me how to load, cock, and fire the gun, and then took me shooting. I had no intention of aiming at anything living, I'd just planned on shooting beer cans or bottles, but there was this robin in the bush at the end of his driveway. He told me to shoot it. I said that I'd rather not, but he said that guns are designed for killing, and reminded me that I'd been the one bothering him for months to take me shooting. "There's the bird, you've got the gun, now shoot it!"

I pressed the stock against my shoulder, aimed, and pulled the trigger. "You missed," he said. The bird flew off, and I was glad that it had gotten away. But it didn't get far. I hadn't missed. Instead I'd wounded it, but not fatally. It flopped around on the ground trying, but unable to fly. "You have to finish it," my friend said. "You shot it and now you must kill it," he said. I stood there with the gun in my hand, suddenly aware of the sunshine, the warm spring breeze, and the sweet smell of blooming and budding flowers, watching the bird flopping helplessly on the ground.

Soon there was another bird flying back and forth frantically between the bird on the ground and nearby trees. "That's its mate," my friend said, as I watched this other bird, obviously upset and not understanding what had happened to its friend. I thought, hoped rather, that the bird on the ground might be all right in a few minutes, but it wasn't, nor was it going to die on its own anytime soon, though it would eventually. "You shot it," my friend said, "You can't leave it there to suffer. You have to kill it." As I stood there I wished I were somewhere else, anywhere else, and that I'd never done this. The robin had done nothing to me. It had been minding its own business, just being beautiful, singing, and contributing to my enjoyment of spring. But I had done this awful thing, and as a result of my actions this bird was now suffering needlessly. "Do it!" my friend said. I tried to get him to kill the bird, begged him even, but he would not, even though he'd killed many birds. This was my doing, he said, and I had to take the responsibility for my actions. In this case, it meant finishing the job. I cocked the BB gun, aimed again, and fired, this time killing the bird.

"Now you must kill its mate," he said, "or its heart will be broken."

"I can't do it," I said. He took the gun from my hand, cocked it, and shot the other robin, killing it cleanly with one shot. I looked at the two birds lying there on the ground and thought how cruel and stupid it is to kill without reason or purpose. I walked home in silence greatly aware of the holiness which I had transgressed, and certain that I would never kill anything again without reason.

I never mentioned the event to anyone, but twenty years later a friend of mine, a full blooded Cherokee Indian and I were walking in the woods one day, and he said, as if reading my mind. "When we are young, we don't understand cruelty. We're cruel by nature. It's only with the passage of time that we understand the way things really are. We are cruel, we suffer, and then, hopefully learn compassion."

I liked the shadows from this candle.

16. THE OLD MAN

I don't remember if I ever even saw him, the man who lived downstairs in the basement of the 1920s house I rented my second year in college. He was old though, I knew that much because I heard him hacking and coughing through the heating system vents in the floor every morning and every night. Of course when you're twenty, nearly everyone seems old, and he was. He left for work early every day, before I was up. I never saw him come or go, and don't know where he went, just that he went to work. The house had been divided into several apartments and, except for the old man, housed students. The basement was no doubt creepy, as it had a very low ceiling and contained the spooky looking gas furnace with its large pipes radiating upward and out of the central unit like the legs of a large, menacing fire breathing spider. As far as I know, nobody ever came to visit him. His life couldn't have been much fun, not that I thought about him one way or the other. I lived in one of the two downstairs apartments with a roommate, a local boy who'd moved away from his parents' house more to party than to study. He and I hit it off and had a good time, although he frequently brought friends over on weeknights who were loud, boisterous, and stayed late. My studies suffered as a result.

We often made a lot of noise, played deafening music, got drunk, yelled at each other, and laughed loudly. The old man downstairs never complained, although he must have found us extremely annoying. One night, in a marijuana and alcohol induced haze, we decided to torment him. My friend came up with the idea of lowering a stereo speaker with loud music blasting, down the vent shaft so that it would be basically right next to him. We did this, turned the system up as loud as it would go without blowing the speaker and treated him to an unwanted concert of some really loud, head banging music. After half an hour or so we tired of this and decided to drop a large amount of uncooked popcorn down several of the vents, thinking that it would get hot and start popping and making noise, which would no doubt bewilder him. We also rattled a chain of some sort down the vent shaft, hoping, I suppose, for him to get angry enough to start cursing us through the vents and give us a good laugh. But he didn't react one way or the other no matter what we did, so after an hour or so of deliberately harassing him without response, we ceased. The next morning I left and returned home to Nashville for the Christmas holidays, and my roommate went back to his parents' house.

Two weeks or so later, I was back at school, and at my apartment. One of the girls who lived upstairs passed me in the hall, said hello, and asked me `if I'd heard about the old man who lived in the basement.' "Heard what?" I asked.

"He died over Christmas," she said. "He'd lived alone and didn't have anybody."

"That's too bad," I replied, and it was indeed too bad that I'd sought to make him miserable when he was really sick. We didn't know he was sick. It was just some pointless prank, I told myself. We were just stupid adolescents having some fun. No harm done. To some degree this was true, but at another, deeper level, I suspected that perhaps, through my actions, I'd lost some part of my humanity.

17. THE GOLFER

I'd just finished an invigorating four mile run on the horse trails at Nashville's Percy Warner Park, and was standing by the water fountain cupping my hand under the running water and dousing my head and face, trying to cool down in the late afternoon heat. I heard him before I saw him, in fact it was his loud stream of profanity which drew my attention to him at all. `Son of a Bitch!' he shouted, `God Damn!' he cursed, and loudly. I felt like yelling through the hedge `Hey, shut the fuck up!' but I didn't. Loud cursing in public usually pisses me off, especially if there are other people around, even though I'm guilty of frequently cursing myself, sometimes loudly, and even in public. But there was nobody else around, that is, he didn't see me, and thought he was alone The cursing continued even louder. Instead of yelling for him to shut up, I moved silently closer to the tall hedgerow separating us and peered through the brush. I was curious. I could see him there in the fading light, about ten feet away, standing next to the green on the fourth hole, practicing his swing. He appeared to be about sixty years old, average height, with graying hair. He bent down and, with great effort, placed a ball upon the tee. He stepped back, took his club and moved up to the ball as if he intended to strike it. But as he raised the club back, at the height of his swing, his hands began trembling violently and uncontrollably. He held the club up for a moment and then swung downward, awkwardly, the club flying from his grip as he missed the ball entirely. More profanity. He walked over to where the club had come to rest, bent down slowly and picked it up, walked carefully back to his golf ball, and went through the motions with the same result, again cursing loudly. I watched this with curiosity at first, and then sadness. Obviously golf was his favorite pastime, but as a

40

result of MS or Parkinson's, or some other acquired malaise, his body would no longer do what he wanted it to do, but still he tried with all his might. Every time he got to the top of his swing he began shaking uncontrollably, and lost his grip. It was obvious to me that he would never play golf again, no matter how much he wanted to, or how hard he practiced. I felt like saying something. Surely there was something I could do to help, but I knew there was nothing I could say or do. I might possibly embarrass him and make him feel even worse, so I said nothing and walked quietly away, unnoticed.

He reminded me of a similar situation in Chattanooga thirty years earlier. I was a student at the time, and chanced to round a corner near the Memorial Auditorium, downtown. There was a girl, about twenty years old, on crutches, standing by herself, crying and cursing. She had just clumsily but deliberately smashed something glass which she had been carrying in a brown paper bag. I heard it break at her feet. I could tell from the shape of her body that hers was not a temporary condition, like a sprained ankle, or a broken leg. This was, had been, and would be her lot in life as long as she lived. I was embarrassed that I had inadvertently and unintentionally intruded upon such a private moment between herself and the universe. But there I was, passing close to her, I couldn't just ignore her. I asked if there was anything I could do, or if she needed any help. She looked at me angrily and said, `Mind your own business!' I kept walking and didn't look back. I felt like a fool for saying anything at all. But what could I have said?

Around that same time, as I listened in class, some English literature professor expounded upon the temporary nature of happiness, and how any unexpected event can suddenly transform one's life from blissful to unbearable. I was young, it was springtime, and I remember thinking that while what he said was probably true on some level, it had nothing to do with me. Everything was beautiful. Within less than two months my world was indeed turned upside down in an instant when I was unexpectedly dumped by my first love. It was the first of several major upsets in an otherwise generally happy life, but it taught me that the world can turn cold without notice. And youth is indeed fleeting.

Those of us fortunate enough to be in good health go about our day to day routines for the most part unburdened by our bodies. Occasionally we see some unfortunate soul in a wheel chair, surrounded by bags, electric motors, monitors, and other devices and we think 'there but for the grace of God go I,' or 'poor bastard.' But it's always someone else, not us, so we soon forget. The fact is that our own health will begin to go at some point, if we live long enough, and we'll witness the young and beautiful in the fullness of life, passing us by, just as we did when we were young. At that point, regrets over things undone become unbearable. If there's something you want to do, or see, or be, or somewhere you've always wanted to go, do it now before it's too late. When your time comes, all of the money in the world won't be able to purchase one additional healthy, happy, or carefree day.

18. CUBAN CIGARS

OK, I admit it. Sometimes I'm just plain lowdown, but I do have a sense of humor. I'd held a mild grudge against the US government for nearly a decade for stealing the Cuban cigars a friend had been kind enough to send me from Canada. Instead of receiving the cigars which my friend had paid for, I'd received a letter from customs or some other government bureaucracy informing me that the cigars which I'd been so eagerly anticipating had been confiscated as contraband. Thanks a pantload!

Anyway, a coworker was accompanying one of our clients to a singing engagement for several days in Chile. I asked him if he'd be kind enough to bring me some Cuban cigars if the opportunity presented itself, although I really didn't expect that he would. When he returned a week or so later, he had indeed brought me two boxes of Montecristo Cigars. I thanked him kindly, for it's a big pain in the ass to lug anything back from South America, or anywhere else for that matter, and through customs, especially when you have your own luggage to deal with.

His gracious gesture was much appreciated, and I was genuinely delighted. When I returned to my office and looked closely at the two bright yellow boxes, I quickly but sadly determined that they were not Montecristos at all, but forgeries, probably designed to sucker American tourists who wouldn't know the difference. The boxes were copies of actual Montecristo boxes, but of much lower quality, and the Cuban government seal was obviously a poor quality Photostat copy. Oh well, perhaps the cigars were good nonetheless. Well, I fired one up, and they were at least made of actual tobacco, and not tree leaves as I imagined they would be. In Nashville, they used to sell novelty 'clown cigars' as I called them at the fair, fun shops, and other outlets on Nashville's lower Broadway which catered primarily to tourists. These were large cigars, and made of tobacco, but not actually intended to be smoked, although technically, they could be. I'd smoked one once late at night when I was desperate for a nicotine fix and all of the stores were closed. It burned like a brush fire and put out a lot of smoke. Well, these 'Cubans' were much like that when I smoked the first and only one of them that I actually tried. I wasn't going to smoke any more of them without a fire extinguisher nearby, if at all.

I began to formulate a plan, which might just work, if I could conclude it with a straight face, that is, without laughing out loud, and actually rolling around on the floor. There was a cigar store in the Vanderbilt University area on 21st Avenue South known as The Oxford Smoke Shop, where I stopped several times a week before work to pick up a few cigars. The store carried a number of my favorite brands, particularly Punch, and Hoyo De Monterey. Despite the many cigars I'd bought in that store during the course of several years, neither the store's owner, or his wife, had ever so much as offered me a sample of any new cigar they were carrying, or might soon carry, as is the practice now, with regular customers at most high end cigar stores. They sold cigars and I bought them. While they didn't owe me anything, a freebie every once in awhile would have been nice. Anyway, I took the two boxes to the owner of the Oxford Smoke Shop and told him that one of our agents had just returned from a trip with singer Brenda Lee from Chile, and had brought me these Montecristo Cuban cigars, but that "as you know, I prefer specific cigars, with dark wrappers, and while these Cubans are mild, smooth, and really exquisite, I

43

prefer stronger cigars. I wonder if you would consider trading me some of my favorites for these two boxes of Montecristos."

He examined the two boxes carefully, withdrew a cigar from the open box, and offered me a store credit of $75 for the two boxes, an offer which I accepted immediately, before he changed his mind. I think the lure of having something illegal appealed to him to some degree, as well as the thought of having some of what were considered to be some of the finest cigars in the world. I'd hoped to get my $75 worth of cigars from the humidor and beat feet before he lit up one of the ones I'd traded him, but alas, this was not to be.

He carefully lit, or rather I should say `ignited' one of the Cubans as I approached the door to leave. It was soon smoking like a Roman Candle. As I stepped through and into the outside world, I turned and smiled, trying really hard not to laugh, as smoke quickly filled the room. I heard him remark as the door closed behind me, "Ah, truly an excellent cigar. Exquisite bouquet!"

Indeed! So long sucker!

This man in this truck was for sale for $100 in a hotel parking lot.

44

19. VETERAN'S DAY

It was late Friday afternoon at the V.A. Hospital. I was there to have my blood taken and thought that the best time to do it was on Friday because by that time most people with doctor's appointments would have already left, and I could get in and out quickly, which I did. It was cold outside and getting dark. I lived about fifty miles away so I wanted to beat feet and I knew I'd be stuck in rush hour traffic regardless, and I had other stops to make before I got home.

As I entered the lobby from the rear of the building heading toward the front door, I passed an elderly man sitting there in a wheel chair. He was a World War II or Korean War veteran, or both, I surmised, judging from his age. He wore some sort of hat, as many older veterans do, a baseball cap with the name of his ship and its hull number embroidered on the front.

As I passed, I heard some woman, a V.A. official telling him curtly that `she was sorry' but there was no place for him in the hospital, that it was full, and that he'd have to come back on Monday and try again. Maybe they could take him then.

He told her that he'd called several times but had reached a recording each time. He thought that something was wrong with him and that he needed to see a doctor. Rather than continuing to get recorded messages for the next several hours, he'd had someone drive him the sixty miles and drop him off. "You should have called scheduling first," she told him coldly. "You need to have whoever left you here come back and get you. I'm sorry, but I can't help you," she said as she walked away. But he had nobody, and there was no one to help him. I should have done something myself. What if he'd been my father? I'd have done something then, wouldn't I?

I was in a hurry, and in a small car. He looked heavy and I couldn't have managed him myself. Maybe I should have called a cab and gotten him a hotel room, but what if there was something seriously wrong with him medically? I've replayed the scene many times, feeling I should have done something to help him. But the hospital probably was the best place for him under the circumstances. Still, I should have started shouting and raised some hell on his behalf. Our veterans deserve better.

1964 Lincoln Convertible. Hollywood, Mississippi

20. JUST SIT ANYWHERE YOU LIKE

'Well, if that happened to me, I know how I'd handle it, ...I'd just...' This sounds good in theory, but the truth is, you never know what you're going to do until faced with a situation. But sometimes an event or circumstance is so totally outside of your everyday experiences that no preparation is even possible.

Here's what happened. I entered the 'Hairless Tweeter' (Harris Teeter) grocery store on Hwy 100, the site of the former Sunflower, also a grocery store, as I'd done thousands of times before. It had been Stevens, Tidwell's, and maybe something else over a twenty plus year period, but always a grocery store. Consequently, I wasn't expecting anything out of the ordinary, let alone anything which could be considered absurd. An armed robbery in progress? A store patron having a seizure or a heart attack? Or a stroke? All within the realm of the possible, even if unlikely.

On this hot as hell summer day, the store's air conditioning offered a stark and wonderful contrast to the heat outside. It was mid-afternoon and the large store was empty except for me and another patron who I was about to encounter unexpectedly. There were some employees at the front of the store behind the customer service desk and at check out, also at the front of the store.

As I reached the back of the store I emerged from an aisle

and walked to the right. I immediately espied some fat bastard, in the quarter of a ton range, that is, 500 pounds or more. At first I thought he might be seated on the floor, that he'd possibly collapsed and his back was propped against one of the refrigerated open gondolas which ran across the back wall of the store. Or perhaps he was seated on a walker or something, since he was actually lower than he'd be if that were the case.

But alas, my eyes deceived me. He was in fact seated on top of the cold cut sections, his ass cheeks spread across the hot dogs and bologna, in blissful refrigerated repose. It took me a few seconds to actually grasp the situation, but no, his ass was in fact perched atop the refrigerated cold cut section. I think I said something, but I don't remember exactly what it was, probably something along the lines of `You filthy, disgusting son of a bitch!"

I immediately went to the front of the store, found a manager and said, "There is some big fat son of a bitch with his ass sitting in the cooler on top of the meat in the rear of the store." He didn't immediately grasp the reality of the words I'd spoken. I'm sure that his training as a grocery store manager did not offer options for such occasions.

My initial shock and disgust subsided as I repeated the tale to my incredulous friends over the next few days. Perhaps he was feeling dizzy, or weak, or possibly on the verge of a heart attack or stroke. Still, he could have at least sat down on the floor, and rested his back against the outside of the cooler instead of actually sitting his ass upon the meat. Maybe, he reasoned that it would take a fork lift to hoist him from the floor. I don't know. I do know that I never bought anything out of that cooler ever again, and as I was in that store on a daily basis, I know I never saw an `Ass Juice Sale' in that department.

I subsequently discovered that the man had indeed had a heart attack and died shortly after this strange event, on the same day in fact. Well, not really. It was just that his ass was hot and the refrigerated meat section was cool and probably comfortable, given the texture of the packaged meats.

21. THE MISANTHROPE
It wasn't the Negroes, the misanthrope was black himself. It

wasn't the new influx of Mexicans. They spoke English, worked hard, and were productive. The problem was white people, not all white people, but the white trash, the hicks, peckerwoods, hujis, and rednecks. They had moved to this small Southern town in ever increasing numbers, over the last two decades, lured by unlimited free government services, including food stamps, housing allowance, welfare payments, and unlimited free medical care. They were as a rule, barely human, feral, actually. They were mostly fat, unclean, uncouth, and in many cases downright ugly. They were also frequently belligerent and often violent, and responsible for nearly all of the criminal activity, including frequent burglaries, stabbings, and methamphetamine production. They drove cars which were in such a poor state of repair that they represented a decided menace to most motorists. Some few of these 'people' were minimally successful financially, and drove large pick-up trucks with giant tires and extremely loud exhaust pipes. Almost all of them lived in trailers, giant sardine cans hauled onto side of the road lots in plain sight, and then surrounded by inoperable junk cars, old washing machines, tires, wheels, and other useless crap.

Their presence was bad enough, but the fact that they reproduced made matters worse. Their numerous offspring were generally dirty and fat as well. Most of the females did not escape high school without becoming pregnant. The males attempted to imitate ghetto chic, wearing stupid-looking knit hats which resembled unrolled condoms, and baggy pants which had to be held in place constantly with one hand. This large group represented the worst of white society. They were not the hard working poor but honest class of people who'd once been the majority of the population in this rural county, the people who'd fought this country's wars, manned its factories, or farmed its land. That group was long gone. These were deadbeats who spent hour upon hour watching television, smoking cigarettes, talking on cell phones, drinking beer, eating junk food, driving around, and throwing trash on the side of the road.

The misanthrope spent most of his days a large, nearby city. There, in the best part of town, he saw few undesirables of any race, and best of all, no hicks. But when he returned to the country they could not be avoided. They were everywhere. At the gas station, at the supermarket, at the drive-ins, and on the road, swimming drunkenly in streams on private land, leaving beer cans and trash in their wake, hunting out of season on private property, and generally destroying the environment. 'Live and let live.' That was the only reasonable policy any intelligent person could reach concerning their presence. As the city sixty miles away expanded, one could but hope the rising cost of land would eventually force these 'citizens' further away into even more rural counties like Lewis and Humphreys. That would take decades, however, and they had to be dealt with now.

The best policy was to avoid them as much as possible and pretend they didn't exist at all. But that was becoming increasingly hard to do. Several events had come together recently which focused on their presence even more. Some hicks had broken the window in his office while he had been out of town for the weekend. They hadn't been deterred by the alarm system, or the deadbolt on the door, or the streetlights. The morons hadn't time to enter the premises, so they had been unable to take anything. They would have had little use for books anyway, but that was not the point. It was that they'd been there at all, like cockroaches or rodents, something you don't want in your house at all because they're filthy. And then he'd been driving down a back road and happened to see a four or five year old girl kicking a dog hard and repeatedly in the stomach while the parents stood by laughing. And then at the store, some fat woman had bought more than a hundred dollars worth of groceries, most of it pre-made junk food, high in carbs, saturated fats, and sugars, as well as several cases of soft drinks, full of artificial ingredients and high fructose corn syrup. She'd entered the numbers on what looked like a credit card, but it wasn't, it was her food stamp card. She ended up paying less than $4. For $105 in basically poisonous semi-edibles. The rest would be paid for by the taxpayer, that increasingly diminishing element of society which actually worked. The idea that these healthy people were buying junk food, at the taxpayers' expense, smoking cigarettes, chewing tobacco, not exercising, and living an intentionally unhealthy lifestyle was bad enough in and of itself. Then they would whine and say they needed medical care for physical conditions brought about by their own activities and bad habits. Animals all!

And then there was the girl at the Piggly Wiggly with two kids paid for by WIC, yet another government program which basically paid women to have children they couldn't afford. The misanthrope felt bad for hating all of these people and resolved that their business didn't concern him. No doubt America was going down the toilet, all civilizations do sooner or later. That's just the way it is. There were probably intelligent people in ancient Greece and Rome lamenting the disintegration of their cultures as civilization crumbled around them. America would no doubt crash and burn, but most likely not before his own time was up. He determined not to be bothered by these hicks any longer and to go about his own business. That was the only way to have any peace in the matter. If he took care of himself, he resolved, that would keep him busy enough. He felt relieved at his decision.

And then he chanced to be inside the Wal-Mart at Waverly, Tennessee, the new `Super Wal-Mart' the social and cultural center of the city, and his resolve melted. There was some Amazon sea hag, some large bovine-looking white woman at least six feet tall, with long frizzy blonde hair. She was big, not fat, not skinny, just big. She was dirty looking and unkempt as she stood there with a cigarette hanging out of her mouth. Her mate, for lack of a better word, was about a foot and a half shorter than she, but also dirty looking. There have always been poor people in the rural South, even through the 1960s there were outhouses and shacks, but there had been in most cases, at least some semblance of nobility. Now there was no real poverty. Even the hicks had multiple color TVs, several cars, food stamps, cell phones, cigarettes and beer, and lived in trailers. The man was skinny, short and rustic-looking, also with a cigarette hanging from the side of his mouth.

As hideous as this pair were, the worst was yet to come. The hag was pregnant. The misanthrope could scarcely contain his horror at the implications. That meant that they had…well somebody, or something, had poked her. The mere thought was nauseating. I mean how?.....Why? The thought was truly pornographic and disgusting. The misanthrope was amazed. What parallel world did these people inhabit? It truly made him dizzy. He quickly regained his composure though, remembering his pledge to merely observe. He couldn't ignore the fact that he had seen these people, because there they were, but who was he to judge them? "I'm not here to judge people, that's not my purpose in life," he reflected, "I do not know their circumstances and therefore am not qualified to judge them no matter how they look. How could I possibly know what has happened in their lives? What misfortunes? What Personal losses? No, God bless them." He turned away and went about his own business.

About thirty minutes later he checked out of the store and returned to his car. There they were again, this odd couple, only now they were sitting in their car, some dull-looking Japanese piece of junk, she in the driver's seat, towering above her mate, with her head nearly touching the ceiling. The misanthrope could see them clearly since it so happened that their car was close to his. He looked at them again in spite of himself. But what were they doing? Nothing, just sitting there silently staring straight ahead into space, just smoking cigarettes. He imagined the neurological activities inside their respective skulls and pictured disconnected wires just sparking, not connected to anything, like downed electric wires sometimes found on the ground after a storm, just sparking aimlessly. In a moment the driver's door opened and the large masculine hand and wrist of this female sasquatch, yeti, or bigfoot, extended through the opening, dumping the contents of the car's ash tray onto the pavement. Dozens of cigarette butts surrounded by a large gray cloud of ash fell to the asphalt. The misanthrope started his car and drove away, having passed this supreme test without comment or judgment, just observation. "The good Lord made them one and all," he said silently to himself, but could not help adding the postscript "but great God almighty, why?"

My favorite painting by an anonymous artist. I was leaving some items at a charity drop off and saw this painting propped against the wall. I persuaded the attendant to let me have it.

22. COKE TO GO

I was returning home from an early spring visit to Florida with my longtime girlfriend, taking the scenic route rather than the truck-laden Interstate. While driving on the old highway, we stopped in some small north Florida town at a fast food joint, and decided to make a pit stop. He must have seen us walk in together, the old man. I'd noticed him, not for any particular reason, but because I make it a point to always be aware of my surroundings, who and what is near me. I waited in the short line while Katye went to the bathroom. After I had received my Coke, I walked over to the condiment stand to get a couple of napkins, and to wait for her. The old man addressed me and said, "I used to have a young, beautiful girl too, but that was back in the war." I looked at him for the first time, noticing him specifically, rather than being merely generally aware of his presence as I had been when I'd entered the area initially. He was around 80 years old, about my father's age, so I immediately surmised that he was speaking in reference to World War II, the understandably defining event of that generation. He was dressed nicely but in a manner that suggested he was, or had been a farmer, that is, jeans, a flannel shirt, and rough lace-up boots. He had a full head of nice white hair, which softened the hard lines of his rugged sun-baked features. He continued speaking, seeking neither my acknowledgement or a response. It was almost a soliloquy.

"That was back when I was young," he continued. "We all had to fight. I didn't want to go, and I hated to leave her, but it was my duty."

"Thank you for your service," I said sincerely, interrupting him briefly. He looked up for a moment and I noticed his steel blue eyes. That generation was more than I will ever be, I reflected, as I looked at his strong and weathered face. "You guys were tough." I said, but he hadn't really heard me, and continued with his story.

"I shipped out to fight in Europe. We wrote each other every day, and planned to marry after the war, that is, if I made it home. A lot of us didn't. We'd put the stamps on upside down," he reflected, "that meant 'I love you.' But one day the letters stopped coming, and then later, I heard that she'd met somebody else. They got married." He seemed as if he were about to cry.

I'd been dumped by my first love and had grieved on and off for ten years. My situation was just as bad in theory, maybe worse. Mine hadn't found somebody else, she'd dumped me on basic principles, generally speaking because of who I am, or was at the time. But at least my pain had ended. I didn't think about her at all, anymore, and really wouldn't have known her if I saw her. I'd had many women in the ensuing years, and finally, ended up where I belonged. I'd concluded that most people do, sooner or later.

Obviously this man hadn't. He'd held on to this disappointment for more than sixty years. I didn't know what to say, so I said the only thing I could think of, "What happened?"

"Well, they weren't happy. They got divorced eventually, and she died. I used to see her around some, but she died. I saw her stretched out at the funeral home, dead. I really loved her."

"Did you ever get married?" I asked. "I mean, did you marry someone else?"

"No," he answered, "I didn't."

I saw my girlfriend emerge through the door across the room, a big smile on her face, and I bid the former soldier farewell. He had survived the war and endured, but I believe he thought about her, his lost love, nearly every moment of his waking life. Even her death could not release him from his sense of loss.

But who was it that he'd really been in love with all of these years? It obviously wasn't the actual woman who'd abandoned him. His love was an imaginary girl, an idea of someone which had been realized briefly once upon a time, long ago. He'd sacrificed his life for an idea, something unattainable. If he could've just released that idea, he might have found happiness in the real world rather than sadness in an imaginary one. In thinking of him now, he reminds me of the obligatory skeletons one sees in a cave or in the jungle in a movie of the explorers who preceded the hero but didn't make it. They're there as reminders that the same road one treads now no matter how remote the terrain, has been taken before by others, who failed to succeed in their quest.

The past is the past, good or bad. It just is. It can't be reclaimed, it must be absorbed, its lessons learned, acknowledged, and then released. One is certainly influenced by it, but it can't be given precedence over the present. Failure to release the past can result in distorted perceptions and rob one not only of the present, but of the future. I determined not to repeat this stranger's mistakes.

23. NIGGER

The word is still used today, though generally in private by white people. It has always been used by blacks among themselves, sometimes in an insulting and denigrating manner, and at other times in an affectionate way. My late yard man, an elderly black man, who ultimately became one of my best friends, used the word nonstop, in reference to anyone and anything, and frequently referred to me affectionately as 'my nigger.' We would always laugh. I never called him nigger though, for I assumed the term had a different meaning for him. But, I'm from the South, and have heard the word used all of my life. It didn't have much meaning to me one way or the other, at least until I was thirty-two years old.

By this time I was successful financially and had flown to north Mississippi one Friday afternoon to buy a 1964 Lincoln convertible from a lawyer friend of mine who was selling it to pay his property taxes. Anyway, there was something not quite right with the brakes and I intended to drive it back to Nashville on Sunday, so we took it to the Co-op first thing Saturday morning to have it checked out. This black man, a co-op employee, jacked up the car, in the parking lot, removed the front wheel, and began adjusting something. There was a lot of activity around us, tractors moving around, and pick up trucks, farmers talking among themselves in this heavily agricultural area. I was standing there with my friend when a man well known to both of us saw us and came over. He was one of the richest men in the county and probably owned several thousand acres. He was also loud and obnoxious. I'd been target shooting with him once, out by the levee a year or so earlier. He'd brought his son along that time, and enough firepower to take over a small nation. His son was about eight years old then, and already had several expensive firearms, one of which had jammed. He'd kept admonishing his son not to "step on his dick!" and cursing him profanely and talking to us about how stupid his son was. I remember thinking at the time how rude and ill-mannered the man was to speak to his own son so derogatively in front of other people.

Today, however, he was by himself, and had driven up in his giant pickup truck, the most expensive and largest one he could find. He was addressing my friend on some matter of local significance, talking loudly, so that everyone would notice him, frequently interjecting the word nigger into the conversation completely oblivious to the fact that this young black man was working on my car literally right next to us and heard every word he said. The black man kept working with his eyes lowered. I was ashamed and embarrassed that this man was so obnoxious. I wanted to tell him to shut his fucking mouth, but he was the kind of person who would have said something loudly like, "What's wrong, don't you like NIGGERS?" and made the situation worse. I held my tongue but I wondered how this young man felt. I wanted to apologize to him to tell him that not all white people are like that loud-mouthed asshole, but I said nothing. I thanked him for fixing my car but he did not reply and would not look into my eyes. As far as he knew, I was one of them too, just some other mean white bastard.

When we left the Co-op and began our beautiful spring day in earnest I asked my friend why Wilson had acted like that in front of the man fixing my car. My friend shrugged and said something like "that's just the way he is." I thought about it all weekend. That person's life was hard enough. Did making him feel less of a person make Wilson feel richer, or somehow more important? It made me despise him. I should have apologized to the man for the words of that loudmouth. I should've said something.

But I hadn't, and that was that. I had a great weekend and drove my car back to Nashville with the top down all the way and had forgotten about the incident. Early Monday morning I received a call at my office from my lawyer friend in Mississippi checking to make sure I'd made it back without incident in the twenty year old car. "By the way," he said "do you remember the young man who fixed your brakes?"

"Yes, what about him?" I asked. "Did he go back and take a razor to Wilson?" I asked, hopefully.

"No, he was in an accident Sunday night on the Interstate near Memphis and was killed."

The word nigger has never had the same meaning for me since that time, despite my sometimes joking around with my yard man. On that dead young man's last full day on earth, his last full day of life, the man who'd fixed my car, someone had intentionally belittled him, tried to make him feel less of a man, less of a person, for no reason other than just to be mean. He'd done it in a cowardly way too, surrounded by his friends, all armed to the teeth, and not having the guts to look the man in the eye and call him a nigger to his face. Tennessee Williams said that deliberate or intentional cruelty is the only real sin. Truer words have never been spoken. But Wilson didn't live much beyond that day either, another year or so and he died from cancer, his many possessions scattered to the four winds in a yard sale and subsequent auction.

A painting by Nashville artist Jack Kershaw

24. GUARANTEED TO KILL

I was sitting in a chair reading a book and smoking an exquisite cigar when I noticed a rapid movement on the floor out of the corner of my eye. My bulldog must have seen it too because he raised one eyelid before returning to sleep. It was a mouse. I'd noticed some of my dog's food pellets in the bottom of my organ speaker over the last several weeks and wondered how my dog, the stupid bastard, had managed to get them all the way over there, across the room. It never occurred to me that I could have a rodent in my house. In any case I determined that I'd take care of the problem the first thing the next morning. I got up early, drove to the neighborhood hardware store and bought some 'glue traps' guaranteed to kill mice efficiently. I would normally have bought a couple of standard mouse traps but with my bulldog staying in the house most of the time, I felt that it was much more likely that he would step on the trap than any mouse, a mouse being possessed of a far greater intelligence.

The next morning I got up and checked my traps. Sure enough, there was a mouse in my trap. The problem was that it was very much alive, but stuck to this piece of thick paper and unable to free itself. It hadn't occurred to me that this was what would happen, that the mouse would be very much alive. I don't know what I had thought was going to happen. When I looked at the box it said 'KILLS MICE' in large, bold print letters. Upon further reading of the package, I discovered that I was supposed to 'conveniently' toss both trap and mouse into the trash. That was convenient indeed. The problem was that the mouse was very much alive and was not going to die other than by starving to death, without further attention. I had to get to my office so I didn't have time to deal with the problem right then. I carefully picked up the trap, mouse and all and gently set it on the floor of my car, determined to deal with it later.

At around lunch time I drove from downtown Nashville to Brentwood to look at an old Lincoln. As soon as I got in the car I saw the mouse and realized that I would have to deal with the issue now. I didn't know what to do. What I wanted to do was to free the mouse and let it go into the residential area where I was going, and that is what I determined to do. I was glad the mouse was no longer in my house but I had no desire to kill it. When I arrived at a suitable place with large yards, away from the main highway, I stopped the car along the side of the road. It had been relatively still up to this point, stuck to the sticky surface and unable to move. I hoped that I could just pull it gently off the surface and send it on its way none the worse for the wear. I picked up the trap, examined the situation and realized that nothing I could do was going to extract the mouse. The trap was flexible, allowing me no leverage to try and pry the mouse loose. The surface was so sticky that the mouse's delicate arms and legs would have been torn from its body before they would have ever been peeled from the surface of the trap. The more upset it became, the more it tried to move, and the more it moved, the more firmly it became stuck to the trap.

I suddenly remembered being six or seven years old when the neighbor's police dog had caught and nearly killed a cat. The cat was on the verge of death by the time we were able to rescue it from the dog, but it was clearly not going to recover. My grandfather had come over and administered the *coupe de grace* so that it would not have to suffer for hours or perhaps days. I remember having been horrified despite understanding what had to be done.

It was now thirty years later and I was faced with the same situation. The difference was that I had caused this to happen. On some level the mouse instantly came to symbolize my entire life, though I didn't realize it at the time, and I started crying uncontrollably. I was successful, had a dream career, plenty of money, and every material thing I'd ever wanted. But I had no feeling for my fellow man, basically considered everyone either an outright enemy or a potential threat, and had run over anybody and everybody necessary to get where I was, or rather, imagined myself to be, at the time.

I cried for that part of my soul I'd already lost, and for the fact that I now had to kill this helpless creature. It had done nothing wrong, it was merely trying to survive. I cried as I looked around for something to crush its head with, apologizing to it for what I had done, the terror I had caused it, and for what I must do now. I finally found a rock big enough to do the job and put it out of its misery. Any further delay would have merely prolonged its agony, and mine. I did what I had to do, left the dead mouse there by the side of the road, trap and all, and eventually returned to my office greatly distraught by the experience, having lost yet another part of myself.

25. RUSH

Fraternity rush was a week long. Basically, new students interested in joining a fraternity were feted at open house parties by the various Greek organizations seeking to enlarge their membership rosters. What I remember so vividly, was the anticipation that Saturday morning. It was the culmination of the week long process. Each of the young men who'd attended the open houses and parties of the previous week had gathered in the large room which was two stories high on the inside with heavily carved gothic wainscoting and arched ceiling beams.

The atmosphere was jubilant and there was a pervasive air of excitement as each supplicant wondered either privately or aloud whether or not the fraternity he wanted to join had decided to accept or reject him. Some were highly confident, and talked boldly about which fraternity they intended to join, others were more somber and reflective, but it was a festive atmosphere. Despite a full week's festivities, some students were still undecided as to which fraternity to join, or whether to pledge a fraternity at all. At length several older male students emerged from the crowd and took their places at a large table which had been placed at the end of the room for this occasion. They fumbled around with a number of papers and multiple boxes filled with envelopes. After ten minutes or so they stood, and one of them addressed the group of would be pledges.

"Welcome, you are here today to pledge one of the Greek fraternities associated with this institution. During the past week you've met members from each of the fraternities. They've gotten to know a little about you and you've seen what they have to offer. By now most of you've probably already made up your mind, but some of you haven't. The way it works is that your name will be called and you'll approach this table and be handed an envelope. Each envelope contains a bid or bids. Some envelopes will have bids from more than one fraternity. Some will only contain one bid, and some envelopes will contain no bids. They will be empty. An empty envelope means that you received no bids from any fraternity. When your name is called, you will approach this table and be handed your envelope. If it contains a bid, you will exit through the main entrance, the front door. If your envelope does not have any bids, you will leave through the back door over there.

"You've no doubt had a good time this past week, but there's more to fraternities than just attending parties, meeting girls, and having a good time. These are people who'll become your friends over the next four years, and beyond. In many cases they'll be important to you the rest of your lives. They'll help you along your way, both here, and later. With that in mind, we want you to sit silently for about ten minutes and reflect upon your decision as to which fraternity to pledge. For those of you who are still undecided, this period of silence will give you a little extra time to make up your mind. This means no talking."

For a few minutes I sat there silently, and then suddenly, and much to my surprise, I was overcome by a feeling of at-one-ment with everyone in the room. I looked at them, my fellow students, most of whom were unknown to me, and I felt a strong emotional bond with them. As we sat there quietly, and it was very strange, it seemed as if this rather mundane event was pervaded by what I can only describe as a sense of holiness, something beyond speech. This lasted about ten minutes and then the spell was broken when one of the young men stood up and called the first name. The student approached the table, was handed his envelope, and then walked through the front door and loudly shouted the name of the fraternity which he was pledging. This process was repeated, but I began to notice that there were a number of persons who, when handed their envelope, left silently through the back door, not having received any bids from anybody. They were not chosen. For the past week they'd visited each of the fraternity houses and put their best foot forward. They'd signed up for rush, had worn name tags, and had wanted to be wanted, to belong, to fit in. But nobody had wanted them.

My name was called and I received my envelope, and looking inside found that I'd received two bids, the one I'd wanted, and another, whose members I'd liked. I walked through the door, one of the chosen, and shouted the name of the fraternity I'd selected. There was loud cheering as I walked toward the group, smiling along the way, but there was no joy beneath my joyful demeanor. I couldn't help but think about how the others felt, those who hadn't been chosen. That brief sense of unity I'd felt with them, for a few moments, and the holiness of it had quickly evaporated and I was left with a sense of emptiness. I was young, and the feeling passed, but the memory didn't. Several years later, a friend's rich father was rambling drunkenly from one subject to another and declared sagely, and without provocation, "I've been accepted and I've been rejected. I've been rejected more than I've been accepted, but then I've rejected more people than I've accepted." His observations seemed humorous at the time, especially since they were spoken entirely extemporaneously, with no introductory remarks, and fueled by alcohol. Maybe what happened to those boys that day, their rejection, was part of their broader education, I don't know. We all experience rejection in different ways and times. Nobody is always immune, no matter how attractive they may be or how successful they become. It hurts, but we absorb it, even if unwillingly. Hopefully through many such experiences we learn kindness, but in the final analysis, my friend's drunken father's words have proven true after all. "I've been accepted and I've been rejected. I've been rejected more than I've been accepted, but then I've rejected more people than I've accepted." In Vino Veritas.

Studebaker in flight Humphreys County, Tennessee

26. SHE CRIED

It was the funeral for the richest man in this small town outside Nashville, and the only funeral home in town was packed. Mr. Wilson had just died from cancer. He could have gone to anyplace in the country for treatment, he certainly could have afforded to go anywhere he wanted, since he was a multimillionaire. But he was 73 years old and, by his reckoning, had lived a good life. I think he just figured that treatment for an incurable disease was more trouble than it was worth, so he spent his last days at a hospital in another small town 40 miles away. His life had never seemed exciting, in fact, he'd lived alone with his mother in the same house all of his life. When she died in her late nineties, he continued living there. He'd attended Vanderbilt University, in his youth, earned a law degree there, but upon graduation returned to his small town, and taken over the family business as the banker in the bank established by his progenitors more than a century earlier.

He had lived in the nicest, though not the largest house in town, but never had anyone over for a visit, and possessed few friends. What socializing he did, and there wasn't much, took place at the bank. His sole recreation consisted of a one week, once a year fishing trip to Apalachicola, Florida. He drove a rusty, beat up Ford sedan as his everyday car, but kept a new

Lincoln Sedan out of sight in his garage. Any ostentatious show of wealth in a small town always creates jealousy and resentment. It's one of the darker aspects of human nature. Mr. Wilson knew this and conducted himself accordingly. His life in this small southern town had doubtless been a lonely one for the most part, given his education and lack of peers. He lived with his elderly mother until she died, and by this time was an old man himself. He never married, lived alone, and seldom spoke with anyone except on a surface level. He was, in reality, a very private person.

I'd met him once or twice, and being interested in nineteenth century architecture, had complimented him on his elegant house. "You are the only person he's ever invited to visit him," a friend observed. I was from Nashville and didn't accept his invitation as I considered it to be one of courtesy rather than something he would have actually enjoyed, although in retrospect, I'm not so sure. He was probably starved for like-minded companionship.

My girlfriend and I had been living in this rural area for a while and I'd come to know many of the townspeople even though I retained my house in Nashville. We arrived fifteen minutes before the actual funeral services began, and found a seat with friends. I saw her, sweet soul that she was, Annie, a thirty year old woman in an eleven year old's body. I'd known her for around fifteen years at this point, and like everyone else who knew her, held her in the highest regard. She'd been tragically beset by brain cancer when she was eleven years old and her development had stopped at that point. She'd bravely, and without complaint, endured many brutal operations, the administering of countless drugs, and had yet, against incredible odds, managed to hold on to her personality, and participate to the best of her ability in the life she'd been dealt. She was well loved by all, and had many friends. She painted pictures, decorated objects, read, studied life, and lived creatively, doing her best to create art in a wide range of media. The disease was progressive and had, however, taken its toll. She now wore a wig, as her beautiful dark hair had permanently fallen out due to radiation. Her speech was somewhat slurred now, but still clearly intelligible, another cruelty of her circumstances. In spite of her relentlessly encroaching illness, she was extremely intelligent. She constantly wore a smile and was very loving, always offering a hug and a kind word to everyone she knew. She was one of those people who literally brightened any room she entered.

In a few minutes, after she'd said her hellos, I saw Annie standing there by herself crying, her small shoulders shaking as she sobbed. I asked her what was wrong and she said through her tears, that she was sad for Mr. Wilson, and she might have been, but I think hers was the monumental and unspeakable metaphysical sorrow of her own condition. I put my arms around her and gave her a hug, and attempted to comfort her, by saying that Mr. Wilson was in a better place. He might have been, but she wasn't. I was sad for her, and cried inwardly as we stood there, but I was more angry at that moment than sad. I was angry that this had been her lot. She'd done nothing to deserve any of this. In this world, horrible people live comfortably and prosper, causing pain and destruction to others seemingly with impunity, and yet here was this kind, innocent girl who'd never hurt anyone, who'd never done a cruel thing in her life.

She lived another seven years or so as her body and organs shut down incrementally. At her funeral, I told her father what a wonderful parents they'd been, and how they'd done such an incredible job giving her the best life possible. I was angry that she'd suffered so much and said so. "Her life was stolen from her."

"Oh no," he said, looking at me with a puzzled expression, "She lived a good life, and was happy."

I've tried to consider her life differently based upon what her father told me that day. I still remember her big smile and her kind heart, but I most remember her as she stood there that day, crying uncontrollably for what should have been but never was.

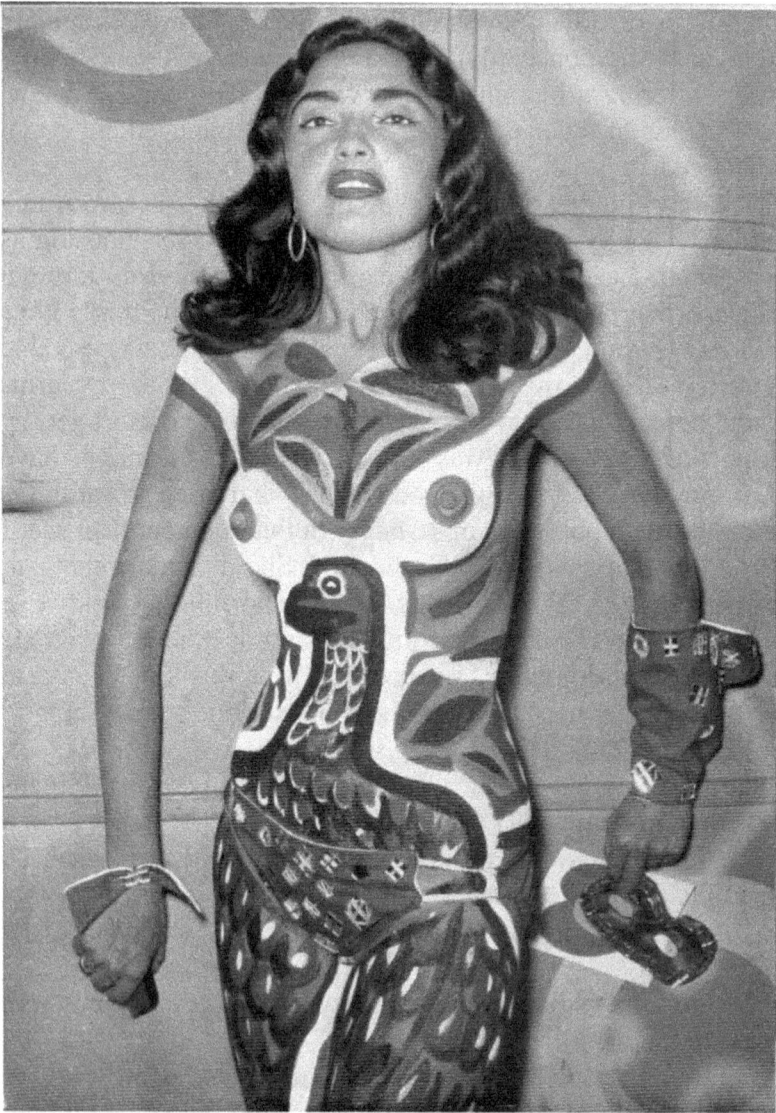

A picture from the book `Le Nuit de Riviera' (1958).

27. THE CLASSROOM DOOR

Nobody particularly liked her, our eighth grade teacher. There was nothing wrong with her per se, we just didn't like her. Perhaps it was her appearance. She was tall, gangly, and awkward looking, and generally unattractive, unlike the other eighth grade teacher, who was young and beautiful. On top of that, our teacher dressed in out of date clothes, not that we had any specific knowledge of fashion, we just knew that she wasn't 'cool.' We were a rowdy bunch, both boys and girls, and did what we could to upset the class and to thwart her attempts at teaching us anything. We weren't violent and blatantly hostile like students in government schools today, but we were intentionally cruel nonetheless, and did everything we possibly could to make her life miserable, without any real reason. One bright, beautiful, breezy, spring afternoon, the classroom windows were open as was the door from our room to the central hall. The teacher stood addressing us, with her hand resting on the doorframe. We all watched silently as the really heavy wooden door moved in the strong breeze from the hallway, back and forth, but ever closer to her exposed hand. This went on for several minutes, and it became increasingly obvious that the door would at any moment close hard upon her fingers, unless she moved them, but she just stood there oblivious to the movements of the door behind her. Nobody said anything, no one warned her. We all just watched. She'd probably move back into the classroom before the door slammed shut, but she didn't. Surely, someone would suggest that she move her hand, but nobody did. Maybe each of us expected some other student to warn her, or perhaps we really didn't expect the door to close, since it had been moving back and forth in both directions. But then there was suddenly a really strong gust of wind and the heavy door accelerated quickly and slammed hard on her fingers. She shouted in pain and surprise and ran crying down the hall away from all of us, an entire classroom full of people, none of whom had been decent enough to warn her. Despite the extreme pain caused by having her fingers mashed in the door, the emotional pain was no doubt much worse. What had she done to anybody that she should be treated so cruelly?

She stopped teaching after another year or so and her husband became a successful attorney, but died early. I saw her once around ten years later but she didn't see me. I wish I could apologize to her now for my part in making her year at my school so unpleasant.

28. A CHRISTMAS STORY

Two young men huddled around an old rusty oil drum in an attempt to warm their hands over the fire. It was hard to keep warm on such a night for the cold wind seemed to penetrate the heavy coats which they wore, and the snow which had been falling lightly most of the day had now started to stick as the temperature dropped. It was Christmas Eve and the two college students were anxious to leave.

It was only six pm and the owner of the stand expected them to work there until 8:00 o'clock or until the last tree was sold. The streets were nearly empty already although there were still a few brave souls stopping by the market across the street to pick something up at the last minute. There were only a few trees remaining and it was very doubtful that any of them would be sold at this late hour.

"What happens to the trees that don't get sold?" asked George.

"I worked here last year," Mike replied, "and there were about fifty trees left over when we closed. Mr. Crownover had us pile them up and a city work crew came and put them one at a time in a grinder and turned them into mulch for part of the trail in some metro park."

"It's sort of a shame," said George, "that a tree would be planted, nurtured, and grown especially to be someone's Christmas tree, and then after having been chopped down and carried in a truck all the way down here from somewhere up north, would not be chosen."

Mike rubbed his hands together briskly over the fire and said, "Yes, it's unfortunate and it seems somehow unfair, but that's the way it is everywhere. It's the same story with pumpkins on Halloween. A good many of them get thrown away. That's just the way it is."

The conversation died away and the two young men stood there rubbing their hands together over the fire, each lost in his own reveries.

"That's life," thought George silently, "Things and people too seem to be fitted by nature for certain purposes only to be thwarted from fulfilling those purposes at the last minute. It's tragic really, and yet I suppose there's nothing to be done about

68

it, that's just the way things really are, yet still…"

A woman in a station wagon came by with her two children, a boy and a girl. They had just returned from Florida that afternoon and bought two trees, a big one and a short one. "I always wait until the last minute," she said. "That way I get them cheaper, and besides, it's exciting to decorate them on Christmas Eve."

George and Mike lashed the larger tree to the luggage rack on her roof and then folded down the back seat and pushed the smaller tree carefully through the back until just the tip was hanging out through the open tailgate.

"That should do it ma'am," George said. "Good night and have a Merry Christmas!" he said.

"And a Merry Christmas to you," the woman replied with a smile. As she helped her two children into the front seat beside her, closed the door, and drove off.

"I think you have to use a real tree to get into the Christmas spirit," Mike observed. "There's just something about it. Maybe it's the ritual of going to get one, you know, comparing them, selecting that one you like best. Maybe it's the fresh clean smell. I don't know."

"At our house we use an artificial tree," replied George. "Naturally I prefer a real one but it seems a waste to sacrifice a beautiful tree to use it for two or three weeks and then just throw it away. Some of those trees if uncut, live to be more than a hundred years old."

"Yeah, I hadn't thought about it that way."

"We used to use real trees like these when I was a kid. Then my father got one of those live trees each Christmas, you know, they have dirt wrapped around the roots in some sort of a tow sack, and you plant the tree outside after the holidays. Since I went away to college my parents have been using the same artificial tree each year and although I didn't like the idea at first, I must admit, it looks pretty good."

At that moment a big 4 wheel drive pickup truck came by and two men bought the next to last tree for a big after Christmas party at a country club next week. There was now only one tree left, so the boss, Mr. Crownover, paid the two young men their wages plus an extra Christmas bonus, and sent them on their way, wishing them a merry Christmas and telling them that he hoped to see both of them next year.

"By the way," he said, "there's still one more tree. If either one of you want it you're welcome to it with my compliments."

"No thank you," they replied, since both already had trees at home.

"The solitary tree stood propped at an angle against the stark and empty wood frame which had been full of trees just two weeks ago. The snow was falling heavily now and Mr. Crownover felt that he'd better leave at once if he was to make it home at all. He folded his tent into his trailer camper, hooked it to the back of his truck, got some water and extinguished the fire in the oil drum. As he prepared to leave he thought to himself that it had been a much better season than last year. He'd sold over a hundred trees this year and several hundred wreaths. This would be a good Christmas for him and the extra money would come in handy. He took a last look around the place to see that he hadn't forgotten anything, and then slipped into his truck and headed home.

George was anxious to get home since his family always had the traditional dinner on Christmas Eve at eight o'clock. Still, he certainly enjoyed the drive home through the falling snow from the comfort of his warm jeep. He reached instinctively for the radio dial but then withdrew his hand, deciding instead to enjoy the beauty of the snow covered night landscape. The snowflakes seemed almost as big as half dollars, and their appearance in the headlights as the jeep approached them produced a dizzying effect, something like driving through the Milky Way might do. Somehow the blanket of snow made everything seem unusually quiet, and the beauty of that solitude was enhanced by the lighted Christmas trees in the windows of the houses he passed.

When George arrived home dinner was nearly ready and it was but a short time until all of his family gathered around the large table as they had done every year as long as he could remember. During the meal itself, conversation was high spirited and happy. At length George's father mentioned that there didn't seem to be as many decorations out this year as there had been in the past. "Perhaps people are more energy conscious now," he speculated.

"I noticed that Mrs. Wallace didn't have her manger scene on the yard this year," George observed.

"Now that you mention it, she doesn't even have a Christmas tree in her front window," remarked George's sister Carol. "I wonder why, her house used to have more decorations than any house in the neighborhood. Is she out of town this Christmas?"

"She used to always make a big thing out of every holiday. She always brought Christmas cookies to you kids. Remember? Every Christmas. Her husband died last year while ya'll were away at school. I thought I wrote you about it. I guess I forgot," their mother said.

"That's too bad, he was nice," George said. "What happened to him?"

"I'm not sure," replied his mother, "he'd been sick on and off for some time."

"She must be out of town visiting her son and his family for the holidays," said Carol, "They live in Texas somewhere don't they? Dallas, or somewhere like that?"

"No, I saw her at the store earlier this week and she said that she was staying in town. Her son is good for nothing. He hasn't visited her in over two years. I don't think he even attended his own father's funeral. At least, I didn't see him there," the mother stated.

"You mean Mrs. Wallace is over there in that big house all by herself on Christmas Eve?" asked Carol.

"Yes, I guess so," her mother replied. "I should have asked her over for dinner tonight when I saw her at the store. For some reason I didn't think of it."

"Mom, you should have," exclaimed Carol.

"Oh, well, it's too late now," the mother answered, "and I think perhaps she'd rather be alone with her memories. You know, Mrs. Wallace and her husband were very close. They loved each other like teenagers, and after all this time. They went everywhere together. You never saw one of them without the other nearby. They always bought each other little gifts all the time. They'd been married nearly sixty years. His death was a sad thing, but life goes on."

"I suppose," said Carol. "It must be horrible to be old and

71

alone."

"That's true," their mother said, "but they lived each and every day to the fullest. Whatever the future holds for her, she at least has the satisfaction of the past. Those two lived more in a single day than most people live in ten years. I'll call her tomorrow and ask her for tea. It's too late to call her tonight."

"I noticed your grades have dropped in chemistry, George," said his father. "You'll never get into medical school that way, son. I think it's that girlfriend of yours."

"Oh no, Dad, she's been helping him. They've been studying biology together," Carol said with a smile.

"That's really funny," George scolded, giving his sister a dirty look.

In another half an hour everyone had left the table and gone their separate ways, to read, watch television, or sleep.

George went upstairs to his room and sat down with a book, lit a cigar, and propped his feet upon the desk. He had difficulty concentrating for some reason. He just couldn't stop thinking about old Mrs. Wallace all alone in that house across the street. Nobody should spend Christmas alone, but what could he do about it? He could maybe visit her tomorrow, but what would he say. They had nothing in common and there was really nothing he could do anyway. He used to cut their yard, but that had been years ago, and besides, old people sort of freaked him out. Still, it was sad. He resumed reading but couldn't keep his mind on it. In an instant he had an idea that might put his mind at ease. He laid his book aside, went to the closet, grabbed his coat and crept down the stairs quietly. If his guess was correct, there was most likely a fairly large box of Christmas ornaments which hadn't been used in the den closet. There always was. It was the same every year, the excess green and red balls, and duplicate ornaments were never used. Sure enough, there it was. George took the box and silently eased out the back door and got in his Jeep. It was still darkly overcast but the wind had died down a bit. The Jeep's wheels made loud crunching sounds as he drove down the long snow covered driveway. He hardly even needed his headlights at all since the presence of the snow made everything appear very light.

George hoped that the last tree which had been left at the

Christmas tree stand would still be there. He hoped nobody had taken it, but there was no way to be really sure without going back there. He could have called Mr. Crownover, but he doubted that he would want to be disturbed, especially after having had to fool with trees for the last two weeks. He really didn't know exactly what he'd do with the tree if it was there, but he'd figure it out. Maybe he should put it on her porch.

Snow had covered everything at the stand, but sure enough, the tree was still there. He pulled into the lot, brushed the snow off the tree, loaded it into the back of his Jeep, and started home. As he drove he felt sort of stupid. "This really is nuts," he thought to himself, "but it's a good idea. I just hope the police don't drive by and see me scurrying around this tree in a neighbor's yard and think I'm up to some adolescent mischief."

George pulled the Jeep into his own driveway, but stopped just inside its entrance. He wanted to do this as inconspicuously as possible, sort of like a commando raid. He hauled the tree out of his Jeep. It seemed bigger now than he'd thought. It was a full six feet tall and very broad at the base. He dragged it across the street by the stand and decided to place it directly in front of a large picture window. He stood it upright and then covered the wooden stand with snow and packed it down with his hands, stopping every few seconds to shake off the cold snow. He stood back and looked at the tree from a distance. It looked pretty good he thought, even though the top was still a little bent.

George next jogged back to his jeep, retrieved the box of ornaments, and then hurried back to the tree. He placed the box on the ground and began putting ornaments on the tree. He laughed out loud as he threw the long narrow strips of foil onto the branches. He knew he must be crazy, but this was fun. In less than five minutes the tree was loaded down with red, green, and blue balls of various sizes in addition to shiny brass stars and smaller items. The tree lacked lights but there was no doubt at all that it was definitely a Christmas tree. "Mission accomplished," George shouted to himself as he lifted the nearly empty box and returned to his driveway at a fast walk. He turned to look at it once again from a point near his house. It really was pretty, he thought although he still felt that what he had done might actually have been either overly sentimental, or downright stupid. In any case, he certainly didn't intend to mention it to anyone.

Christmas morning was cold but the sun came out early and in full force. George and his family opened their presents first thing in the morning as they'd always done. In the house across the street, Mrs. Wallace slipped on her robe and descended the stairs. She tried to think of this as just another day. She tried to avoid any thoughts of Christmas altogether, but they came anyway. Everything she saw evoked painful memories. There, in the corner, is where the Christmas tree was placed each holiday season for all those years. She could easily imagine her husband sitting there in his favorite chair wearing his red slippers and smoking one of his pipes. Everything in the house brought back memories of their life together. She sat down in his chair and wept openly. "Why God? Why?" she asked the empty room through her tears. "Why did you take him from me? He was all I had in this world. You knew that. Why? I'm so alone," she thought "So alone. Help me."

Bye and bye the crying stopped and she slowly opened her eyes. Somehow, she felt calmer now, as if someone or something was comforting her in some vague but powerful way which she did not understand, yet could not help but acknowledge. As she sat there vacantly staring through the closed curtains, something on the other side caught her attention, a reflection of some sort. She stood and tugged the string which parted the curtains. The light she saw was reflected from one of the ornaments on a beautiful Christmas tree which now stood in front of the window. As she gazed upon it, her husband's words returned to her. "Remember not to worry, no matter what happens to me, because I'll be with you wherever you are and whatever you do. I promise. I will always love you. You know that." As she stood there in silence looking at the Christmas tree glistening in the bright sunlight, she knew that his words were true and realized that although she would probably always be lonely, maybe she would never be alone.

29. ONE BRICK TOO MANY

I remember the first time I saw him, a Hispanic looking kid with grease on his hair. He was quiet, well dressed, and intelligent, a new friend of my son's who was also a student at the so-called magnet school. Joseph was the boy's name. He must have been about twelve years old at the time. I was glad that my son had a new friend, and since I like individuals of all races, I was glad that he was broadening his horizons. I took them both to The Great Escape, a used record, comic, and trading card store in Nashville. Somehow I got off on a tangent about magnet schools and about how it wasn't right that the hard working students ended up in some crappy run down building in the midst of the government projects, while the deadbeats got to go to the nice schools in the nice neighborhoods. The magnet schools had no tennis courts, no football, or baseball teams either. This is not how life works in the real world, I told them. The non-productive fall by the wayside and the deadbeats end up on the bottom, living off the labors of others. I was in rare form, preaching to two twelve year olds. I dropped them off, picked them up a couple of hours later, and then returned them to my ex-wife's apartment complex.

Later, that evening, my son called me up and explained that I should not have said the things I'd said, because his friend Joseph lived in the projects, his mother was on welfare and food stamps, and it wasn't Joseph's fault. He was just a kid. Truer words had never been spoken. I was both embarrassed and ashamed. I'd hurt some kid's feelings, to me an almost unforgivable sin. My error had not been intentional but had produced the same results nonetheless. I was disgusted with myself. I asked my son what I should do. Should I call the boy and apologize? No, I was told, you've done enough already. I had disregarded two essential rules of conduct. I'd assumed that since the kid was at a magnet school he was from a prosperous family, as most of the students were, a `good' family. I had violated the number one rule of conduct `Don't assume anything. When you assume, you make an `ass of you and an ass of me.' Number two, be sure that the mind is engaged before putting your mouth in gear. Why couldn't I have just kept my damn mouth shut? But I hadn't. He was a good kid. His circumstances clearly weren't his fault, and he'd made the best of them so far, overcoming incredible odds, studying hard, and avoiding the all too frequent pitfalls of poverty and life in the projects, circumstances which I could only imagine.

The boy and my son remained close friends for the next four or five years, and I did what I could to atone for my ignorant insensitivity in the ensuing years, including apologizing. Eventually, they were roommates together at a state university, both on academic scholarships, but here their paths ultimately diverged. My son received several bids from fraternities, but Joseph did not. He dropped out of school eventually, and didn't graduate, and they lost touch. My son made other friends, and so did Joseph, and Joseph got a job as a stock boy at a drugstore chain but didn't seem to be moving in the right direction. Although he maintained his strong work ethic, he became a victim of bad association and was also involved with a young woman who broke his heart. In desperation, and with a strong desire for survival, he joined the army, seeking somehow to reorient himself and get his life back on track. The service has helped many young men get squared away, refocused them, taught self-discipline as well as provided a trade. Two weeks before Joseph was to leave for boot camp, however, he killed himself. If he could've just made it another two weeks, his whole life would have changed completely, and for the better, but he couldn't see that from where he stood. His entire existence had been an uphill struggle from the day he was born, and yet through sheer tenacity he'd succeeded in spite of every obstacle fate had thrown in front of him. The breakup with his girlfriend was the final event, the one thing he couldn't get beyond, in a life that had been beset with hardship. He was too young to understand that things do get better, but had no point of reference from which to view a happier future. The load he carried had finally become too heavy to bear.

30. I'M FINALLY A MULTIMILLIONAIRE

I'd known him since I was six or seven years old. We'd been in Cub Scouts together, but there were periods of time, often years, during which I didn't see him at all. He was from a rich family and was an only child. He'd had everything given to him, not that I resented him. He was a friend of mine with a great sense of sarcastic humor. Like most of us, he'd been forced by his parents to work in high school, not that he or they'd needed the money, but so that he would learn a solid work ethic. We were back from college, he from Texas Christian University and me from a small college in Chattanooga, and had met for lunch at a semi-fashionable restaurant where he'd been forced to work for a time as a bus boy. On his last day there, he'd stuffed his hat and apron into the commode in the men's room and flushed them, overwhelming the system and flooding the restroom and part of the corridor. The waitress, an elderly woman, remembered him and spoke to him at the table. "Well Clark, what have you been doing?" she asked. "I've just returned from my studies at Oxford," he replied. This off the cuff reply, a complete fabrication, delivered with a straight face caused me to laugh out loud.

He went to law school and moved to Savannah with his wife,

bought an antebellum mansion there and I didn't see him for awhile, that is, until his father's funeral. I'd stopped by his parents' house for a visit and he said, in front of his mother, "I'm bored, do you want to gang bang my wife?" I told him to behave.

Not long after that, he had some type of brain aneurysm and almost died. A couple of years later he was divorced, back in town, and had bought some 1910 mansion in a decaying part of town. He complained to me that he'd put on a little weight while he'd been in Georgia. I generally ran around fifteen miles a week during this period, and advised him to do the same. "You should exercise I told him. Are you going to walk around on eggshells the rest of your life waiting for another aneurysm to hit you? Hell, get with it," I told him.

By this time I was married and working on my career in the music business. We'd meet downtown for lunch frequently and sometimes go to the gym together. He told me several years later that my advice had changed his life. He looked great and was fit. I thought, "That's the worst advice I've ever given anybody. He's lucky it didn't kill him."

One winter it was really cold in Nashville and the temperature didn't exceed zero for two weeks. I was going through a divorce myself and just wanted to get away. He was the only person I knew who had no pressing commitments and could afford to go anywhere he wanted without notice. I called him and asked him if he wanted to go to Haiti next week. I told him I was going to Key West for the weekend and would meet him at the Miami airport at a certain time and that we'd fly to Port Au Prince, and go from there. I halfway expected him not to show, but there he was at the airport when I arrived. We had a great adventure for two weeks and it was a trip I'll never forget, for many reasons.

Eventually he moved across the state line into Kentucky and bought some early 19th century Federal style two story mansion. After that I didn't see him at all, unless he came to Nashville to visit his mother, who was a family friend of my own mother's. His visits to her were rare, and his calls to me even less frequent.

We lost touch. His mother eventually died, and my mom told

me about it and said that I should go by the funeral home and pay my respects. I did, and my friend and I stepped out onto the front porch and visited while he smoked a cigarette. "I'm sorry about your mother," I told him, to which he replied, "Well, I'm finally a multimillionaire." It was a strange thing to say, but I thought, maybe now he would buy a decent car. He was the cheapest person I've ever met, despite the fact that he'd had a Mustang, and then ordered a brand new Oldsmobile 442 to his specification, while still in high school. Then he got a Mercedes Benz SL, and a new Porsche, while still in college. Now he was driving some beat up ten year old Toyota station wagon, despite the fact that he was already rich. I couldn't understand why he was so cheap. He hadn't been that way in high school, college, or afterward. It started when he moved to that old house in the middle of nowhere. Basically he'd lost touch with all of his friends and started drinking, stopped exercising and basically abandoned the real world. He'd wanted to become an author and sent me some things he'd written. They were similar in tone to some of Henry Miller's early work, and I thought, quite excellent. I encouraged him but told him he'd have to buy a computer and type his work to make it presentable. He replied that "computers were expensive." I told him that he could afford to buy as many as he wanted and that if he intended to be a writer he'd have to submit a properly prepared manuscript. Instead of buying a computer, he gave up writing.

He treated his longtime girlfriend like shit for twenty-five years, but when he'd had to have some hip replacement surgery, she'd been with him throughout the ordeal, basically without sleep for several days. I saw her at the hospital after his surgery, while he was still in recovery. I hardly recognized her. Twenty-five years with him had used her up.

I'd always enjoyed our time together and considered him one of my closest friends, even though I'd not seen him in several years. We spoke occasionally, and I'd send him a book I'd written from time to time. Then, one day he called me at my house in Mississippi. As soon as I answered the phone, he started telling me how disappointed he was in me. He'd caught me off guard and I reacted angrily, without even giving him the chance to speak any further. I quickly told him that he'd been sent to the best schools, given money, clothes, cars, and houses all of his life, and hadn't accomplished anything.

He listened quietly to my rant and then hung up the phone without saying anything further. In looking back, I think he'd intended to tell me that he was disappointed that I'd never taken the time to make the fifty mile drive to his home, given our long and mutual love of antebellum architecture, but I hadn't given him the chance.

I don't remember whether he called me or I called him, but we spoke several days later and I told him how wrong I'd been to say what I'd said, and that it wasn't true. He replied, "There's no reason to end our friendship over this." I told him that I would always be his friend regardless, and that I was truly sorry for my outburst. It was my fault.

One Sunday morning about a year later, I received a call from a former mutual friend, still a friend of mine but no longer of his. She told me that my friend had killed himself the previous afternoon. A single pistol shot to the chest. He'd called me on the Thursday before his death, I guess to say good bye, though I hadn't known it at the time. We'd had a long and pleasant conversation. And now he was dead by his own hand, and I would never see him or speak with him again. I sadly recalled the mean things I'd said to him that one time, and I now remembered that he'd invited me to see his house many times over the past ten years and I'd never gone to visit him, not even once. I'd always been too busy. He never gave any indication that he needed anything from anyone. He had no problem with sarcasm himself and readily dished it out, often cruelly. He always had. Still, I never suspected that he might have needed me to actually be a friend, or that he might have needed help. Did my cruel comments help push him over the edge? I'll never know. I know I'm sorry for what I said, and that I miss him. He'd been my friend for fifty years. I arrived late at the graveside service, having finally come to visit him, in the middle of nowhere Kentucky, but ten years too late.

31. I'LL SHOW YOU

She was a bright, young black girl, a typical teenager, with plenty of attitude, but, as with most adolescents of her age and era, nothing to back it up other than her own high opinion of herself. Her uncle is a friend of mine, in this small, rural community, sixty miles west of Nashville, where everybody knows everybody else, so I found out what happened quickly. Quite simply, it was a typical Friday night, and the girl wanted to go to a party. Her mother had refused this request inasmuch as the girl's schoolwork was not up to par as of late, and she'd started hanging around with people who were, in her parents' estimation, not of the highest caliber. She was under age and there would doubtless be older boys there, and likely alcohol and marijuana as well. It was just not a good situation for their daughter. She was told why they'd reached their decision, and that she could do whatever she wanted when she became an adult. In the meantime, as long as she lived at her parents' house, she was expected to abide by their rules. That meant she was to go to school, study hard, stay out of trouble, respect her parents, and to do what she was told.

But none of that mattered. She wanted to go to the party anyway, and that was that. She pleaded, reasoned, bargained with her parents without success, and then, still failing to persuade them to her way of thinking, screamed and yelled her disapproval of their 'stupid rules.' "We aren't here to be liked," her father told the girl. "We're here to raise you. You don't have to like what we tell you to do, but you do have to do it. That's just the way it is."

"Then I'll show you!" she shouted as she stomped up the stairs to her room. After about an hour she stumbled down the stairs, barely coherent and foaming at the mouth. "I'm sick Momma. Help me," she cried.

"Tina, what have you done," she shouted, taking her daughter in her arms and helping her to a chair.

"Child, what have you done? She asked again fearfully.

"I took some pills Momma. I'm sick."

"The girl's father called for the ambulance, and the paramedics arrived quickly. They did what they could to stabilize her, but by the time the ambulance reached the hospital, it was too late. She died in the emergency room, the result of a senseless, and needless tragedy.

Everyone in town was upset by what happened, but life goes

on. "At that age," her uncle reasoned, "they don't know anything. They see some actor die on TV and then see him on another show two weeks later. They must really think that actions have no consequences. I guess on some level, she thought that she'd make her point, that her parents would see that they were wrong for not letting her go out that night, and that everything would return to normal like nothing happened. She made her point, I just don't know what it was."

32. TOM

I'd always liked Tom though I didn't really know him that well. We were both in the same business, and both successful. While there is indeed a certain unspoken competition between all talent agents it was nothing specific. His acts, like my own, were American icons, each unique and each famous. I'd known him since the early 1970s. He was already successful when I entered the business as a junior agent. I'd visited him at his office once and noticed a large, solitary Seeburg studio monitor speaker sitting on the floor in the hallway. I asked him about it and he told me that it had come from the Mercury Records Recording studio. I had one just like it, told him where I got it, and he confirmed that mine was the 'other one.' I asked him if he'd sell me his but he declined. I offered to flip him for it, meaning a toss of a coin. If he won, he'd get my speaker. If I won, I'd get his. In either case, one of us would have the complete pair. Again, he declined. Finally, a couple of months later, I traded him a new nickel plated Smith & Wesson 357 Magnum pistol for his speaker, and the pair, were again complete.

By the 1980s I'd moved up in the entertainment business world and was head of my own company. But Tom was extremely lucky, some folks just are. Everything he touched turned to gold. It was amazing, almost like he'd made a deal with the devil. I mean everything he did worked. For example, one of his employees brought an act to Tom's talent agency. The employee left to pursue other interests, the act was subsequently signed to a major record deal and became famous. The act's original manager was sent to prison for something illegal, so Tom more or less inherited the act. I used to use this act of his as the opening act for one of my major entertainers at auditorium shows before they became superstars. Since both artists were on the same record label, and my act was already famous, I was able to buy his act for $1,000 a night. The record company picked up the difference and subsidized this up and coming group, feeling that the fastest way to bolster their rising record sales was to put them in front of the large audiences my star already commanded in major arenas and concert halls.

My act in this particular instance was shortly eclipsed by his, who ultimately became one of the most awarded acts in the history of recorded music. The act stayed with him for nearly thirty years before retiring, making him a multi-millionaire many, many times over. My act was a constant problem for me, left my company and returned, threatened to leave, left, returned, and left again. Tom's act stayed with him the entire time, knowing that the wealth and fame which they'd achieved were based not only upon years of hard work, but also upon incredible luck. As this act's career was winding down, Tom ended up with another up and comer who became a superstar, again, almost by accident, as if this new client were yet another gift from above.

Tom was a nice looking guy too, handsome actually, with an outgoing personality and a big smile. His mistress was equally beautiful, although she was also married. He eventually set her up in business and made her rich as well. She ultimately got divorced but stayed with him until she retired and moved to California.

I remember driving down Music Row one morning and a beautiful new Rolls-Royce pulled up on my right. It was Tom in his brand new black Silver Spur. I was amazed. It seemed that God smiled on everything he did. I wasn't jealous, I've always been inspired by the success of others, incited to work harder, longer, and smarter. I eventually got my own Rolls-Royce, but mine was an antique, a black 1948 Silver Wraith with an aluminum Freestone & Webb body. It was elegant, but his was cool, sleek, and new. He'd also bought his wife a new black Rolls-Royce convertible with red leather seats.

Anyway, I hadn't seen Tom in several years and was downtown at a deli and saw him speaking with someone across the street. He didn't see me, the traffic was bad, and I was in a hurry, so I didn't try to flag him down. About a week later I ran into another friend who mentioned Tom's incredible luck and how he'd lucked into one of the hottest acts in the music business, again, almost by chance. I said, "Yeah, he must have made the same deal with the devil that Garth Brooks made. Who knows?" We were both mystified. Again, this isn't to say that he wasn't both hard working and capable, he was, but so were we. In addition, Tom was just lucky.

Another year or so elapsed and I ran into another music business friend, this time in Belle Meade at Starbucks. I hadn't seen Eddie in a while either. I'd known him for more than thirty years had worked with him, gotten him jobs, he'd worked for me, I'd worked for him, I'd sued him and won, fired him, stolen acts from him, and on one occasion put him out of business altogether. We were still friends despite our rich history, perhaps even because of it. As we stood there talking he mentioned Tom for some reason, he'd worked for him many years ago, and I knew they were still friends. I asked how Tom was doing. He said' "Haven't you heard?"

"Heard what?" I asked.

"His son killed himself."

"How did it happen?" I asked in stunned disbelief.

"He shot himself in the heart right in Tom's back yard."

"Why?"

"Well, he left a note. It said that he kept hearing his father's voice telling him to kill himself."

"Jesus Christ!" I said, "That's horrible." I couldn't believe it. I remembered seeing his kid driving around in a 1959 Ferrari convertible. I assumed Tom's son had the world by the ass. I also remembered that the kid had knocked up a friend of mine's daughter, and had heard that Tom would have nothing to do with his own grandchild. I'd thought at the time that that was sort of unkind, especially since the girl's father was well known and fairly well-liked. Things like that happen. It's no longer the disgrace it once was, thank God. I didn't know the details so I really didn't have either an interest or an opinion. His loss, I figured. One should have a relationship with one's own grandchild, but it was none of my business.

"I don't think he ever told his son he loved him," Eddie observed, in an uncharacteristically rare expression of unguarded emotion.

I thought of my own son, whose best friend had killed himself at twenty years old three years ago. What an unnecessary waste, and for nothing. I also realized that things aren't always what they seem. Those who seem so outwardly blessed on the surface often live very different lives privately. Sure, I would like to have had Tom's success, but under the circumstances, I'm thankful for what I've got, and truly understand that there but for the grace of God go I. Nobody ever knows what's going to happen or when. I would rather have my son alive and happy than all the success and money Tom ever achieved. It is the people in my life who matter to me, my friends and family, who make my life exceptional.

33. WHAT GOES AROUND

David was an aspiring singer, and probably the worst person I've ever known. He didn't actually kill anybody. Instead he fed off their energy. He was horrible. Of the people in his immediate circle during the year and a half I wasted fooling with him, one had a heart attack and died. Another had a heart attack, but survived. Another was fired from his job, and his wife got cancer and died. Another man got a divorce and lost his business. Another woman lost her job of twelve years. Additionally, he had the truly unique ability to bring out the absolute worst in everyone he ever met. Anyway, I had a Cadillac convertible, a big, dark blue 1976 Eldorado, the last of the real Cadillacs. Well, it wouldn't do but that he had to have one too, and it had to be better than mine. Sure enough he got one from his home town, someplace in New Jersey, and had it shipped down to Nashville on a truck by some insured transport company. He called me as soon as it arrived and I went over to his apartment to see it. It was black with red leather and a white top. The paint was original and in perfect condition. So was the leather and the top. It was definitely` better' than mine, which is what he wanted, not that I particularly cared. In transit however, there must have been a car on the hauler above his, because some oil or transmission fluid had dripped onto the trunk lid of his car and slightly discolored the paint. It was noticeable, but just barely. The damaged area was about the size of a quarter.

He was furious and vowed to make somebody pay. In retrospect I believe now that he was working himself into a state of self-induced righteous indignation to justify the con game he was about to perpetrate on the carrier's insurance company. He raved about how his original car would never be the same now that this damage had been done by the negligent car transporter. I assured him that it was no big deal. "Just get them to pay to have the trunk lid repainted," I said. "It won't cost more than a hundred dollars at most, and they'll probably pay for it."

But he'd hatched a plan that he would demand $5,000 because the entire car would have to be stripped, taken down to the bare metal. Otherwise, he reasoned, the paint on the trunk would not match that on the rest of the car. It was more than that, he explained indignantly. They had also somehow punctured the top as a result of their carelessness. Well, actually he had punctured the top himself, he explained. It wasn't much of a puncture, like maybe an ice pick would do, but he wanted that money, and had worked himself up to the degree that he wasn't committing fraud, he was just getting what he had coming as a result of the damage `they' had done to his car and the stress and inconvenience this had caused him. "It was like they did this to me intentionally," he told me. It's not a lie if you believe it, and he believed it now, having twisted it around in his cunningly dishonest mind.

I told him that what he was contemplating was not merely illegal but unethical. Since he literally had absolutely no sense of right or wrong, he actually did not understand my misguided advice, my attempt to dissuade him from his plans. It was like I was somehow against him too.

I stood my ground, but he went ahead, nevertheless. He browbeat, harassed, threatened, and intimidated the insurance adjuster so thoroughly that to my surprise, they sent him a check for five thousand dollars. The car was not worth more than $7,500 at the time. He felt vindicated. His car would never be right, of course, but at least he'd managed to stop the transport company from 'putting one over on him.' He'd done nothing other than protect himself from one of those 'greedy corporations.'

What he did was pocket the money and find somebody out in the sticks who agreed to take the car down to the bare metal and refinish it better than new for $1,500. In other words, in his greedy self-absorbed mind, he figured that he was getting paid $3,500 to have his car repainted. He'd pocket the extra $3,500. But as they say, what goes around comes around. Things didn't turn out quite like my friend intended. He'd paid the body shop owner a $500 down payment but work had not proceeded as expected. The car had had all of its chrome removed, the side strips, the front and rear bumpers, and the door handles. The body had been stripped of all of its paint and covered in flat gray primer. It was a mess. To make matters worse, the car, which was supposed to have been kept inside the shop, out of the weather, had instead been unceremoniously left in the gravel driveway area outside the corrugated metal building, exposed to the elements.

It was at this point that my client asked me, as a Southerner, and a hick, to intercede in his behalf with the shop owner to see if I could persuade him to finish the job. I discovered that my client had promised the body shop owner that in exchange for a lower price, he would help do much of the work himself, using the grinder and sander in the laborious job of removing the old paint. He'd actually worked for about three hours the first day and that was it. Of course he neglected to tell me that he'd agreed to all of this at the outset. He'd failed to mention any of this. I visited the shop owner on his behalf and got the entire story.

At this point the shop owner was willing to start to work again, as agreed, as soon as David paid him another $500 as originally agreed, since the money was to be paid incrementally as work progressed. The other thing, the shop owner said, was that the car's owner would have to come back and work, as agreed, that meant physical labor, not standing around watching while somebody else did the work.

Though David had, in fact, agreed to do the majority of the work himself, he balked at doing anything additional, having experienced a few hours of real work for the first time in his life. He didn't intend to pay the shop owner any further money for ruining his car. He would get a lawyer and sue the shop owner for substantial damages. So he sought several lawyers, seeking to find one who would work for nothing other than the honor of representing him. In the meantime, David had been brave from a safe distance, calling and harassing the shop owner several times a day, but the fact was, David was scared of the shop owner, who was tough, skinny, and fearless. By the time I paid the shop owner a second visit his attitude had changed much for the worse. "I'm not going to finish the car for any amount of money, and I'm not going to release it until he pays me for the work I've already done. I hate that son of a bitch and if I see him again he might have an accident. All those pumped up gym muscles don't mean shit to me. He's never done a real day's work in his life. If he calls me again I'm going to fuck him up. I hate that yankee piece of shit."

I agreed with him, because he was right. I'd come to hate the son of a bitch myself for being who and what he was. I personally hoped the shop owner would ruin the car.

Three weeks later, after telling me about the situation several times a day, David decided that the best thing to do was to get the car out of that place as soon as possible. He'd been unable to find a lawyer who was willing to work for nothing. I agreed to let him store the car in the driveway behind my house for a couple of weeks until he decided what to do with it. Of course he had to pay the shop owner an arbitrary 'storage fee' since the shop was no longer working on the car. It ended up costing David another $1,000 to get the car back, $1,500 in all. What a shame. I asked David if he might see some connection between what had happened to him and the fact that he had basically stolen $5,000 from an innocent party through a false insurance claim. He saw no connection at all and was angry that I would even suggest that he had done anything unethical. "That's not the kind of person I am. I was just seeking a fair compensation for the damage to my car. C'mon, you saw the damage that transporter did to my car."

In the three week interval that the car remained at my house, he found another body shop willing to take the car, who would fix it as good as new for $2,500. The car was towed from my house and the next time I saw it, it looked almost as nice as it had the first time I saw it, only now, or course, the paint was no longer original, thus reducing the car's value. It had turned out fine after all, David reasoned. The car would have had to have been stripped down anyway. Since that had already been done, the new body shop was charging him less that it would have if it had been necessary to start from scratch. He'd still managed to pocket a grand for his trouble, and still have the car repainted.

In the meantime, he continued working against me, seeking to undermine the work I had been doing on his behalf, as his manager. He was driving me crazy and not making me any money. I went to a friend of mine for advice, the manager of one of the most successful and enduring acts in country music. He asked me if I seriously thought David was going to make it, to become a star. I told him that the singer was probably the most talented act I'd ever represented, even though I had represented some of the most successful acts in American music, a fact of which he was well aware. I mentioned that I had him under contract. My friend advised me to drop him as a client immediately and not to look back. "If he is as bad as you've described him, it's unlikely that he'll ever make it anyway, and even if he does, imagine what he'll be like then. You're better off without him, even if he does make it. You've had many acts, you'll have many more, but ultimately you can't make a good deal with a bad person."

I weighed his words carefully and released David from his contract with me. It turned out to have been a wise decision on my part. He never made it as a singer, despite his incredible talent, because of his self-destructive nature. He actively attempted to cheat everyone who worked in his behalf, even before there was any reason to do so. Everyone who knew him for more than two weeks actively hated him. He was that bad. His actions behind the scenes reminded me someone deciding to steal the silverware as the Titanic was sinking. He's the only person I've ever actually fantasized about killing.

As to the car, it was fixed again as I related, but then, one day downtown, David had illegally parked it, since the law did not apply to him, and a city bus came flying around the corner and destroyed it, crashing the back bumper all the way to the back seat. He still didn't see any connection between his thievery and its immediate consequences, but as they say, what goes around comes around. It really couldn't have happened to a nicer person. And he never did make it as an entertainer. Ah, sweet mystery of life.

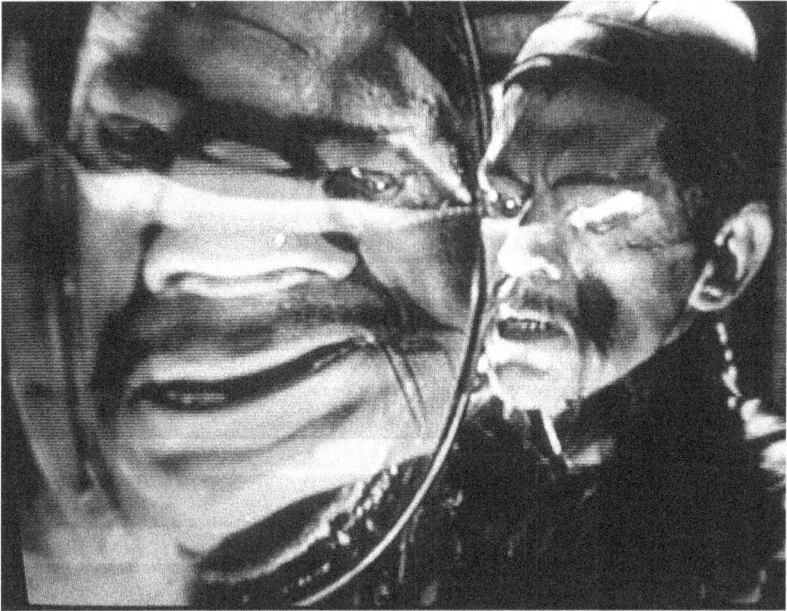

34. BLACK FRIDAY

I've always hated gutters. More specifically, I've always hated cleaning gutters. Anyway, there I was lying on the ground with the paramedics crouched over me, doing, I don't know what. Strangely, it didn't matter what they did. It was like I was somehow detached. I was sort of above myself, just watching them at work, but it was me all right, and for some reason I didn't care what they did. The ladder was lying there on the ground next to me where it had fallen, where we'd both fallen when I'd reached too far and it had twisted, and we'd both hit to the ground. "We're losing him," I heard one of them say. I knew that they were talking about me, but for some reason, I didn't care.

The next thing I remember was the light. I had a sense of dizzying acceleration as I was whisked through some type of tunnel or chute, toward this bright light. And then I was in a waiting room, like at a doctor's office. As I remember, everything seemed really bright. There were other people there waiting too, although none of them moved or said anything. I'm not sure how long I was there, but it wasn't long. Someone called my name, I stood up, and she escorted me into an examination room and told me, "He'll be with you in just a moment. You may be seated while you wait." I guess that she meant the doctor would soon be with me, but she didn't say.

I didn't have to wait long. There was a knock on the door and then the door opened and there I was face to face with Elvis Presley, the king of rock n' roll. It was him all right, and not my imagination. "Bob, I'm Elvis Presley," he said as he smiled at me, extended his hand, and greeted me warmly. I stood and shook hands with him, feeling for the moment like the luckiest person in the world. It was really Elvis. How cool is this? "Is it really you?" I asked. "But you're..."

"I assure you that I'm here and so are you," he smiled, and told me to sit back down.

"Bob," he asked, again calling me by my name, "do you know where you are?"

"Not really," I answered, not that it particularly mattered.

"You've had an accident, do you remember what happened?"

"Not really. I think I was doing something outside. It's the Friday after Thanksgiving, I know that because Susan, she's my wife, was going shopping, and I was planning to…I was going to clean the gutters."

"That's right," he said, and directed me to look at some sort of large television or video monitor of some sort, which he activated, by some method unknown to me. I mean, it seemed to turn itself on. "Take a look," he said, "this is your life."

He sat there in a chair next to me just watching this movie about my life. It was very interesting and I recalled many things I'd forgotten, as well as a lot that I remembered. I saw myself as a child, building model cars, swimming in the creek, having

Thanksgiving dinner, playing baseball in high school, learning to play piano, and then guitar, laughing with my friends. I saw myself crying when my dog was hit by a car. Then I was at my grandfather's funeral in Kentucky, and then at Ole Miss, which I didn't finish. I saw myself singing with my band at fraternity dances, and sometimes drunk, and making an ass of myself. And then I saw myself reading the paper about Elvis Presley's death. I was twenty two at the time, back in 1977. Like many people my age, I'd felt this sense of extreme personal loss, as if I'd actually known Elvis, as if we'd been close friends, although I'd never met him, that is, until just a few minutes ago. And now, here I was, sitting next to him watching some movie about my life. It covered everything, I mean nothing was missing. It was all in real time, but the movie itself didn't seem that long, maybe about fifteen minutes. I laughed and I cried, feeling everything just like it had been when it had actually happened. It's hard to explain, but I was watching this movie about my life, but was reliving it too. It doesn't make any sense telling you about it now, but I understood completely. The movie ended with me getting halfway around the house, falling off the ladder, and then stepping into the waiting room. At that point, the screen went blank.

"What do you think?"

"Am I…am I `dead' ?" I asked him.

"Yes and no," he replied, looking at me seriously for the first time. "It's really up to you. Well, it's up to both of us. When we were watching your movie just now, did you see anything you would like to have changed in any way?"

"Yes, I saw plenty that I'd have done differently, given who I am now, things I'd like to redo. Is that possible? Do I get a second chance? Is that why I'm here?"

"No, it doesn't work like that. You've made mistakes, but you've learned from them. I made mistakes in my time, and I'm stuck with them, just like you're stuck with yours."

"But Elvis, you did all sorts of good and unselfish things for people. You were always buying somebody you didn't know a car, and giving money to the poor, often on the spur of the moment, doing things for people you didn't know. And you never bragged about it. Most of it was under the radar. A lot of the good that you did only came to light after you died."

"I knew what it was like to have nothing. My family was poor. I came from nothing. I understood how it felt to look in the windows of the Memphis department stores like Julius Lewis, and Goldsmith's, and to know that I would never have the money to buy anything. I didn't want anybody to feel like that. That was part of it, I guess. But to make someone really happy, someone who had no expectations of anything and to see their faces. That was my greatest joy."

"You seemed unhappy, but you must have been happy at one time. When it came out that you were a drug addict I thought that the press had made all of that up, and I hated them for it, but in time it became obvious that it was the truth. But I still don't understand the drugs. Why Elvis? You had everything."

"Bob, it just happened. At first I took pills to keep me going, you know, for energy. Nobody really knew anything about the damage they caused back then. And then I took other pills to help me sleep. At first I was young and happy, especially when I bought that first house on Audubon. Everything that happened to me was wonderful. I had everything I wanted... girls, cars, money, fame. Everything. I got to `be Elvis.' After a while though, it became a burden, and I didn't know why any of it had happened to me. Everybody wanted to see and be seen with `Elvis.' Everybody wanted something from me, but nobody really knew me. I know that sounds trite, but fame is never a blessing. It distorts your perceptions, and that's what happened to me. I no longer knew who I was. I saw pictures of myself, and read articles about myself, but it was like they were about somebody else. It wasn't me. But we're not here about me, we're here about you."

"So I really am dead, aren't I?"

"Yes, you are, at the moment."

"But what about the pearly gates and all of that? Is there some sort of judgment day? I'm not ready for that, just now. There are things I want to change. Is it really too late for me? I'm genuinely thrilled to meet you, even under these circumstances, but I'm beginning to have some misgivings about being here."

"What's done is done, like I said, but, everyone has his own destiny. I had mine and you have yours, and that's the reason

I'm here, to help you. Let's look again at the screen and see how things are right now," he said.

The ambulance was driving down the street rapidly and there I was, or at least there my body was, lying on a gurney, with my wife sitting beside me crying. Suddenly, where I was mattered to me for the first time since I'd fallen off the ladder. I had to take care of her. That was my responsibility, that was why I was alive in the first place.

"This is horrible," I said, "please turn it off. I can't stand to see this. Please!"

"The accident was an accident, Bob. Things like that happen. The reason that I'm here with you now, is that the powers that be in this realm, given your particular circumstances, thought that you'd be likely to relate better to me than to somebody else. When I died back in 1977, you dropped out of school and decided to become an Elvis impersonator. I'm truly honored by your tribute, since most of my impersonators reflect what I like to refer to as my 'Dracula' period, when I was, let's face it, fat, dressed in polyester and routinely sang crap like 'Suspicious Minds,' and 'In The Ghetto.' In terms of my career, those weren't times that I remember fondly. At least you chose to represent me at my prime for your portrayal, and you've done a credible job. I do appreciate the thought, but the truth is, and this is why you're here, you have your own life to live. You can't be me and shouldn't try. You need to be yourself. I've been dead three years now, and you're nearly thirty years old. It's time that you find your own destiny and make your own mark in the world. Are you with me? Do you understand me?"

"Yes, I do. I see what you mean," I told him. And I did. I'd been making money, and playing regularly, but realized on some level that it wasn't going to last forever. It really was time for me to get back on track, and on with whatever it was that I was supposed to do.

"That's good. You're still young, and bright and I think you've got the message. Are you with me? Are you with me? Bob! Bob!"

Suddenly, I was on a stretcher in the ambulance with a throbbing pain from the back of my head all the way down to and through both legs, and the paramedic was aiming a flashlight in one of my eyes and shouting at me. "Bob, are you with me?"

It's been, let's see, twenty-one years since that happened to me. I returned to Ole Miss, graduated, and eventually got a real job in Nashville. I know this sounds strange, but that's how I met Elvis.

35. GAS STATION

I'd stopped to get gas for my car on Poplar Ave. in east Memphis, before driving back to my home in north Mississippi. I'd been in Memphis all day, and was more or less out of money, having gotten what I needed from my bank in the morning. I walked into the station, paid the attendant, and returned to the pump. There were four separate gasoline pumps at the island where my car was parked, one of several situated in the large asphalt lot. This gas station was located on a main route in a fairly prosperous part of the city. Nevertheless, when I returned to my car, there was a man, perhaps 40 or so years old, bent over, with his arm extended as far as it would go into a nearby trash can, a few feet from the rear of my car. I watched with curiosity as he withdrew a small open Styrofoam container which someone had discarded. There was a fork still in it, so he immediately used the fork and took a bite of whatever residue was still inside the container. I was appalled that he would eat something like that, not even knowing what it was, or how long it had been there. He must obviously be drunk, crazy...or truly hungry. As I put gas in my car, I watched as the man was quickly approached by a woman in her thirties, waving a $20 bill as she drew near him. This is good, I thought, imagining that she planned to give him the money. He certainly needed it. Instead, she asked him for directions, turned and left, without giving him the money, or anything else. After she walked away, the man turned to me. He was very thin, with a weathered face. His right arm appeared swollen and was bright red, as was his right hand which did not appear to work. He was clearly neither drunk or crazy, as he spoke to me, but I really couldn't understand him since his voice was so soft. I told him that I couldn't hear him and asked him to speak up. He was asking me for money. I had just spent what money I had on gas, except

96

for some I needed to get some medicine on my way home. I told him to wait, that I had some money in the car. I only had $3 over and above what I actually needed, and gave that to him. If I'd had more I would have given it to him.

It's difficult to imagine that there could be somebody that destitute in this country, a place where people routinely pay $4 for a $ .50 cup of coffee. There are plenty of bums around, drunks, deadbeats, and the lazy who have chosen begging as an alternative to work. This man was clearly not in that category.

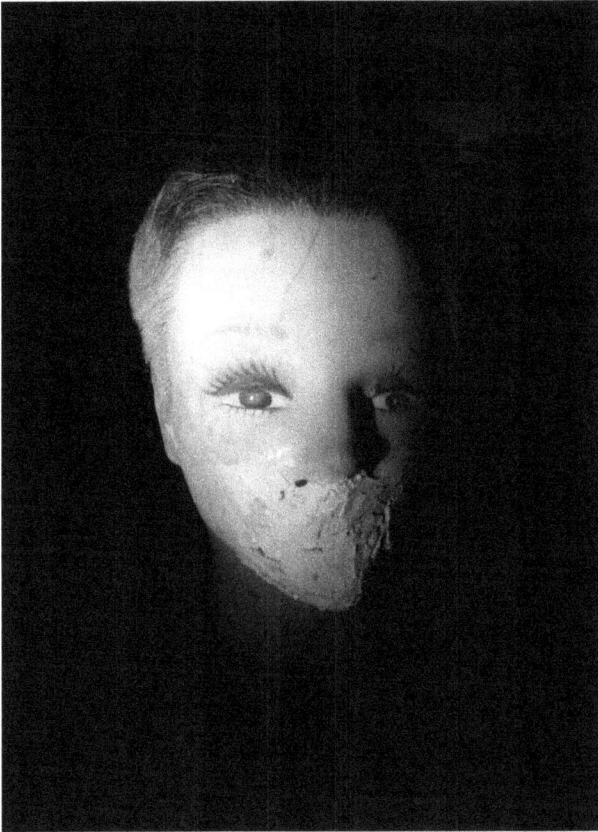

36. ON THE BRIDGE

It seems to me that I was ten or eleven years old at the time, but I can't be sure. What I do remember is that it was a bright, warm, early spring day, and I was happy. I was at the boat dock's restaurant at some fishing camp at Tennessee's Woods

Hill Reservoir having my favorite meal, a cheeseburger and French fries. With me were my mother and her friend, the late Dr. Ballard, a well-known and respected Nashville surgeon. The three of us were ostensibly on a fishing trip.

These fishing expeditions were not infrequent, although as I recollect now, my father had been brought along on the first one or two, probably to establish that that's all they were. Dr. Ballard was a college friend of my grandfather's at Northwestern, and they'd both ended up years later in Nashville and maintained their friendship. He was a frequent guest at our house, and was over for dinner at least once a week, and always around at holidays. In fact, he would often show up in Daytona when we were there with my grandfather. He was at least 20 years older than my mom and was still married, although his wife had looted their checking and savings accounts and taken his two daughters and moved to Arizona ten years or so earlier. He'd sold his large two story house on fashionable Golf Club Lane and now lived alone in a downtown hotel room to be close to his office.

The cabin at the boat dock where we stayed had two bedrooms, and Dr. Ballard and I had occupied one of them, and my father and mother, the other one. Everything was, after all, above board. I liked going fishing whenever I could, especially in the summer when I got to go salt water fishing in the Halifax River behind my grandfather's house at Daytona Beach, Florida.

After my father went once or twice, that was it for him. He wasn't into fishing, so he stayed home after that. Actually, as I subsequently ascertained, I was being used as a chaperone, or should I say, cover, for their trysts, although I hadn't known this at the time. My father was not with us as his presence would have hindered their efforts, and he didn't like fishing anyway, and knew that I did. He'd asked me about the sleeping arrangements once, and I'd told him. Dr. Ballard and I slept in the same room. I also mentioned that I'd wake up from time to time during the night and he wouldn't be there.

I liked Dr. Ballard. He was nicer to me than my father was, and he was a dynamic self-made man who'd come from nothing and become rich and respected. I remember this particular trip because while we were eating, someone came running excitedly into the restaurant asking if there was a doctor anywhere, saying that a boy had been fishing off the bridge and had between crushed between two cars, but was still alive. Someone inside the restaurant approached our table and asked Dr. Ballard to go with the man. Dr. Ballard always had his medical bag with him, and I knew it was in his car. I thought that he'd jump up, get it and rush to the bridge. To my surprise, he replied calmly, "I'm not that kind of doctor." I was horrified that he would do nothing to help this boy who turned out to be my age.

Word came back to the restaurant fairly soon that the boy had died. I didn't want to see him lying there dead on the bridge so I didn't look too closely. I did see the man who'd run into him and killed him on the bridge. He was highly distraught and inconsolable, crying loudly. It had been a tragic accident. I felt horrible for his sorrow and for the dead boy and his family. It had been a beautiful spring day that had gone terribly wrong. I couldn't believe that Dr. Ballard had refused to help. When I'd asked later why he hadn't, my mom told me that it was too late for the boy on the bridge and that he was going to die anyway, and there was nothing Dr. Ballard could have done to help him. Yes, that may be, but how could he have known that without having seen him? I asked. She didn't have an acceptable answer for that, but said that he didn't have his medial bag. I replied that It was in the car, to which she said that he didn't have anything in it that could have saved the boy, and there was the possibility that if the boy had died anyway, Dr. Ballard could have been sued.

My pal Termita lives to ride and rides to live!

37. THE THREE PUPPIES

I was on my way to Florida on June 15th, the day after my marriage as well as one day after my birthday. I was in a jubilant mood to be en route to Daytona Beach, since I had spent so much time there as a child. Just south of Atlanta on Interstate 75, I chanced to look to the side of the road at just the instant that three small puppies followed each other onto the right lane of the highway. They were immediately run over and killed by a car pulling a two wheel trailer, all three of them. It had happened that quickly. In a matter of seconds their lives had come to an end, before they were even old enough to have had any concept of life, or death.

38.   ATTEMPTED MURDER

"Your mother can't help you now," she screamed angrily as she held me in both hands and shook me as hard as she could. "She's dead and she's never coming back!" Her eyes were black with rage and the veins at her temples stood out like writhing snakes

100

just beneath the skin on each side of her contorted red face. It was a hell of a thing to say to a little girl. I didn't know where my mother had gone, she'd died when I was less than two years old, but I knew now, even at four years old that this woman was crazy, and dangerous, and a lot bigger and stronger than me. She would always do this, shake me as hard as she could, and shout mean things at me just as soon as my father left for work. This would frequently be followed by her grabbing me roughly by my arm and half lifting me and dragging me to the hall closet, shoving me in there and closing the door behind her. I felt safe in the closet and would lie down and press my face against the cold floor. I knew that she couldn't see me in the dark, and if I was lucky, she'd forget about me for awhile. Under the sofa was another safe place for me since she was too lazy to bend down and look beneath it. I was so small that I could I'd hide there. She'd stomp around the house calling out my name, not because she was concerned about my whereabouts or my safety, but from pure rage. I would close my eyes as she passed by screaming my name and I would silently ask God to help me.

I knew that I was alone and on my own, and thought that at some point, sooner or later, she would probably hold my head under the water as she bathed me and drown me and that there would be nothing I could do to stop her. I also knew that since she was an adult, everybody would believe that it had been an accident. After all, who would hurt a child? But if I killed her first? I knew that it would be even less believable that a four year old would or could have murdered anybody.

I'd done nothing to her to make her so angry with me. That's how I knew she was crazy. She really would kill me sooner or later, I was certain of that, unless I took some sort of preemptive action. The sooner the better. But she was bigger, stronger, and smarter than I was. One summer night while we'd been visiting some friends of my father, as I was walking around with my small bottle of liquid soap, making bubbles by dipping the round wand into the jar and then blowing through it, I got an idea. This soap bubble liquid was very slippery. If I killed her first, I'd be ok. I laid down a patch of this slippery liquid where I felt she was likely to step, slip, and hopefully die. As I'd hoped and intended, she did indeed slip, and she fell…hard. Unfortunately, she'd been carrying one of the children to bed when she hit the hard floor and he broke her fall, and also his arm.

My last memory of her was of me flying through the air when she'd literally thrown me at my father in the middle of one of their heated arguments. Fortunately, he caught me, but after this incident, he finally divorced her, which probably saved my life, or hers.

39. MAKE A WISH

We were in New Orleans at Brennan's for lunch one bright spring morning, and seated in a semi private dining room. In a few minutes he entered the room with another woman, and was escorted to a table for five and seated. Nicholas Cage. I recognized him at once, having seen several of his movies, most notably '8mm.' I'd heard he had a place here, so I wasn't surprised to see him. Everybody famous gets to New Orleans sooner or later. Shortly thereafter, three women joined them, all smiling. One of the women, introduced herself, and her two companions as he stood to greet them. I am so and so, she stated, giving her name, "of 'Make A Wish.'" She then introduced another person, and a pretty teenage girl who stood beside her on crutches. I'd heard of 'Make A wish' and knew that it was a charitable organization which granted wishes to dying children, but I'd never known anything beyond that. Obviously the girl's wish had been to meet her favorite actor, Nicholas Cage.

Cage stood and greeted them warmly as they were escorted to his table, taking each one's hand as it was presented, and repeating her name as he smiled and telling each in turn that he was happy to meet her.

The group were afforded their privacy but we were seated close to them and while not eavesdropping, it was impossible not to hear much of what was said. They all ordered from the menu and talked pleasantly among themselves. Throughout their time together, Cage expressed genuine interest in the pretty teenage girl, whose blushing shyness diminished after a few minutes, as indeed her wish was being realized. At one point Cage stood, went to her and presented her with a beautiful ring of some sort. She beamed as she opened the box and he placed the ring on her finger.

This was not about him. There were no photographers or press people there, and it wasn't about boosting his public image. It was an act of genuine kindness, something he could do for a stranger, another human being, a person he'd never met, and likely would never see again. He did it because he could. This happy day would live in that girl's memory as long as she lived, and his exemplary kindness will be remembered by me as long as I live. Compassion is indeed the vice of kings.

Nicholas Cage's gift to this dying girl reminded me that we all have the ability to brighten someone's day with a smile, or an unexpected compliment. This is especially applicable to those we see in the same places every day, the bank teller, the checker at the grocery, or the mailman. They're there all day every day, doing the jobs they do, work which we often take for granted, and yet very much depend on. Often we run around, seemingly nonstop and just don't think about it, but we do each have the ability to make somebody else happy every day. And we should.

I've since learned a lot about 'Make A Wish,' and the wonderful work it performs, and the real happiness it brings to people and families who are in hopeless circumstances. I encourage you to check out 'Make A Wish America' and to contribute to their mission of bringing joy where it would otherwise not exist.

40. BOSS MAN AIN'T GONNA LIKE `AT

When I moved to the country 40 miles west of Nashville, I was bored...at first, but there was a 1969 or 1970 Lincoln MK III which had formerly been bought new by the father of an acquaintance. It had found its way to the so-called Lincoln dealer, T & A Motors. I thought I might buy it, as I'd had Lincolns all of my adult life, among other cars, but had never had a MK III. When the two door coupe first debuted in 1969, it was Ford's answer to the 1967 Cadillac Eldorado, a successful two door coupe which had redefined the American luxury car, and had been touted as a `personal luxury car,' that is, a very large, elegant two-door coupe with a powerful engine and visually striking lines.

This particular MK III had seen better days but still looked presentable in its original light cream color with nice tan leather. It was an impressive car even now, 25 years later.

I called the Lincoln dealer and spoke with the man in charge and told him that I'd possibly be interested in the car, and asked if it was ready to go? He replied that he thought the battery probably needed charging, and to give him a couple of hours. We set a time, and I arrived precisely at the appointed hour only to find that somebody was washing the car. This wasn't Jamaica. To me an appointment at an agreed upon time means precisely that, not some vague, but later hour.

But before I proceed with my tale, let me describe the dealership. It was something from the Andy Griffith Show. There were a couple of new Lincoln sedans and a few new Ford Explorers and a couple of new Taurus wagons, not much of an inventory. They were haphazardly arrayed on sort of a semi-paved gravel and grass parking lot in front of the, uh...showroom? It was nothing to me one way or the other, just curious. Maybe there wasn't that much business in that part of the county. But when I opened the front door, I literally had to step over a large sleeping hound, and then walk around another one. Where were the bales of hay? I felt as if I'd mistakenly wandered into the Twilight Zone set of 'Hee Haw.' I didn't mind and I like dogs anyway, it just seemed strange.

No salesmen rushed to greet me, instead I was directed as follows by a janitor: "You've got to see Bulldog. That's who you've got to see. You've got to see Bulldog. He's the salesman." I inquired as to where I might find 'Bulldog,' and was told that he was on the premises and would be around 'directly.' I imagined the arrival of a large stocky ex marine of the Viet Nam era with a flat top haircut and the stub of a smoldering cigar hanging out of his clenched teeth, somebody who looked like General Patton. By and by Bulldog sauntered into the room, a tall, gangly wisp of a fellow with thinning blonde hair topped with a large straw hat, not a panama, or an optimo, but something one would use when cutting the yard. He was fashionably attired in a white polyester suit with matching vest and trousers. This was his domain and he was clearly comfortable therein. He explained proudly that the car was outside, and indeed ready to go.

He motioned me to the driver's side with a graceful wave of his arm, and settled suavely into the passenger seat. I turned the ignition key and was greeted by a very loud grinding sound as the starter engaged the flywheel. "It kind of sticks sometimes," he said casually. "Try it again." I did, and the big 460 V8 roared to life. I noticed the fuel gauge was pegged all the way to the left, indicating that we'd be lucky to get out of the parking lot.

"Oh it's all right," he said, casually dismissing my concerns, so I started out of the parking lot and down the highway toward town. Immediately the car began hesitating and sputtering, and I knew that it was absolutely out of gas. I managed to coast to the side of a pump at the Exxon station. It took Bulldog, myself, and a couple of gas station employees to push the nearly three ton car the remaining six feet or so distance to the gas pump.

Bulldog bought $3.00 worth of gas and we both got into the car again, none the worse for the experience. The car wouldn't start at all this time. He got out of the car, opened the hood and shouted some instructions. With the hood all the way open, I couldn't see him or hear him, so I opened the driver's door and leaned around, with my left foot on the ground, my left hand on the steering wheel, my right foot on the gas pedal and my right hand poised to turn the ignition key.

"All right," he shouted, "try her now!" Nothing. Some banging and clanging followed as he smacked something under the hood with a hammer, something I couldn't see at all. "All right, try her again, but this time put her in neutral," which I did.

As soon as I turned the key the engine roared to life and the car immediately, and without warning, jumped into reverse of its own accord. When it did, the open driver's door struck a lamp post in between the two gas pumps bending the door all the way forward, parallel to the front fender before I was able to stop the car's rearward movement. I was lucky as hell that my leg hadn't literally been torn off, so I was understandably pissed off by what I correctly perceived to be 'Bulldog's' bland nonchalance and colossal incompetence.

He shut the hood, pushed his farmer's hat toward the back of his head and surveyed the damage, stating as he scratched his head perplexedly "Boss man ain't gonna like 'at," to which I replied with some irritation, "Boss Man should've had a mechanic replace the starter to begin with, and Boss Man should have had enough gas put in the car for a test drive before I arrived. And what kind of dealership doesn't have its own gas pump on the premises?" I got out of the car, and myself, Bulldog, and a couple of the gas station employees managed to at least force the door back in the direction it needed to be, but there was no possibility it was ever going to close again without major surgery.

I saw the once beautiful car parked forlornly behind the dealership several times over the course of the next few months, unrepaired, unmourned, and abandoned. Then, one day, it just wasn't there. I didn't see it again for several years and hoped that someone had bought and repaired it. Such, however, was not the case. One day as I drove down the airport road to take off the trash, I saw it parked next to a large abandoned former factory, awaiting one final ride, its transportation to the scrapyard one county over to the west. I stopped and looked at it and was saddened by the state into which it had now fallen. Not only had the door never been fixed, but the once beautiful tan leather had baked and cracked from exposure to sun and water, and its vinyl top was shredded into strips, and the metal beneath rusted. The rest of the car was mostly either covered with mildew or eaten away by rust. I took some pictures, and that was that. Two days later as I passed, it was no longer there, a truly tragic end for such a once magnificent car.

41. THANKS FOR GIVING ME A CHANCE

We were in a hurry, in Memphis, having to meet someone with a truck about ten miles away who was going to pick up 12 antique chairs we'd bought and follow us to Holly Springs, Mississippi, about forty miles south of Memphis.. We were running late, and I didn't know whether the truck was a pickup or what, whether or not it was covered, or what the driver looked like, and rain appeared likely. But Katye wanted to stop at some discount store on Summer Avenue en route.

It seems as if there is always some bum hitting up people for money nearly everywhere I go these days. Begging has taken the place of jobs, mainly for nonproductive people who are basically paid by the government to get out of the way so that the country can still work. The Mexicans, Chinese, Indians, and other immigrants have gladly taken the jobs that they formerly had and have used them as stepping stones to prosperity. Since many of these are not beggars, but potential robbers, depending on circumstances, I'm always aware of who and what is happening around me when I park, get in or out of the car.

Basically, I have a right to go about my business without being accosted or bothered by somebody hitting me up for money. There is always the possibility of being robbed or murdered. I love Memphis, but it's a violent place with blacks killing each other and robbing others at an alarming rate. There's usually at least one murder a day there, at least, and many more shootings, the majority of which are committed by black people. The reasons for this are perhaps debatable, but the reality isn't.

I'm not responsible for their problems systemically or individually. On the other hand, something needs to change. Consequently, my reaction or response depends on my mood, and/or the circumstances at any given moment, and ranges from 'What do you need?' to 'Beat it!'

Anyway, there he was, a young black man with dreadlocks, and a red polyester jump suit. I noticed that he was accosting everybody in the parking lot, approaching them for whatever reason. There was a bulge in his front pocket which could have been a pistol, as was the bulge in my own pocket. I had no intention of letting him get close enough for me to find out. As he approached me I said to him loudly "I'm not interested, I don't care what it is!"

He said "God bless you," as he walked away, "and thanks for giving me a chance." It was not said snidely or with sarcasm.

But I hadn't given him a chance.

As he approached someone else, I saw that he had a stack of CDs in his hand, that he was selling the music that he'd made. I knew he had no other outlet, and didn't have access to anyone who could move him to the next level. He was willing to get out and work against incredible odds to overcome the many obstacles in his way.

If my money hadn't been in the car, and if I hadn't been in a hurry to meet someone ten miles away, and if it weren't for all the black on white crime in Memphis, I might have given him a chance. Better safe than sorry, but I was sorry. I looked for him again the next few times I was out that way, wanting to apologize and buy one of his CDs, but I never saw him again.

42. THE MEETING

By this time, my company, In Concert, had gone the way of all fish, to paraphrase Sammy Butler, a famous author in his day, and I'd joined the former World Class Talent Agency as an agent. Anyway, all of the agents were scheduled to meet in the conference room with former Oak Ridge Boys singer William Lee Golden, who at that time was no longer singing with the group, although he would later rejoin them. The purpose of this meeting was ostensibly to listen to his ideas and to work on scheduling meaningful and profitable performances for himself and his current band, and the meeting was to be conducted by Terry Cline, a former agent from the former Jim Halsey Agency, a formerly Tulsa, Oklahoma based company which had long, but now formerly, represented the Oak Ridge Boys. (The word 'former' frequently applies to nearly every aspect of Nashville's music business).

Terry Cline had a long standing relationship with William Lee Golden, stemming from Golden's long years as a member of that former gospel group the Oak Ridge Boys, which, after many personnel changes had become immensely commercially successful when they changed their 'floormat' as some music business workers used to phrase it, from gospel to country, in the mid-1970s.

Anyway, Terry Cline intended to be all business at this meeting, considering it to be serious stuff. I, however, was in one of my 'moods' for lack of a better word, and rightly concluded that Cline, as the big cheese, would be seated at one end of the long table, and Golden at the other, with agents on each side of the table. In anticipation, I'd repositioned the comfortable chairs around the long conference table to suit my own purposes, so that one particular chair was at the far end of the table, opposite where Cline would be sitting.

Since all of the chairs were identical in appearance, it was impossible to visually distinguish the 'defective' chair from the other six or seven identical chairs, without actually sitting in it and leaning back hard, at which point, the back of the chair would slowly tilt backward. And I mean really backward, though almost imperceptibly at first. After it reached a certain point, however, if you didn't sit upright immediately, it would flip over entirely. The chair seemed innocent enough, at first. You sat down, rested your back against the rear seat back leaning against it like you would in any comfortable armchair. The chairs were 'plush,' so to speak, and comfortable, unlike most rigid conference table chairs. I'd only become aware of this particular chair when Cline had sat in it once unawares, and slowly and constantly had to adjust his position to keep from falling over, an event I witnessed with great mirth. Seemingly, he'd forgotten the incident, but I hadn't.

William Lee Golden arrived at the appointed time and was escorted into the conference room where we were all waiting. After greeting everyone, he took his seat at the vacant chair at the end of the long conference table, as expected. He tried to maintain his rather quickly diminishing equilibrium almost instinctively, yet not consciously aware of his actions. The seat back of the chair would give a little more with each movement or gesture, however slight. At length he realized that something was up with the chair, but apparently nobody in the room noticed it. None of the other agents knew what was going on as the meeting continued, just me. Their ignorance of the situation made it that much funnier to me, and I began smiling at first, then chuckling quietly as my face grew redder with each passing moment.

In short order, I began seriously losing control. I bit the inside of my lip, covered my mouth, coughed, fidgeted, trying my best to think of something...anything other than that slowly collapsing chair, and its collapse was imminent. Finally, others started noticing me, and staring at me, and of course that only made it worse. I knew that at any moment, without warning, I'd start screaming like a hyena. It was inevitable.

Thinking quickly, I stood up, covered my mouth and coughed, saying, "Please, excuse me, it's my allergies. I'm sorry." and indeed my face was red and tears were running down my cheeks and my chest was heaving. My excuse was credible under the circumstances. I immediately went to the men's room and laughed loudly and hysterically for at least fifteen minutes before emerging red-faced and teary eyed retaking my seat as if nothing had happened. But it had. It was one of the funniest things I'd ever done, although it was neither understood nor appreciated by my colleagues.

Abandoned house. Knoxville, Tennessee

43. I THOUGHT I SAW A GHOST

I generally ran three miles a day, usually before lunch, on a measured track, where I could consistently time myself. This was usually at Vanderbilt University, which was near my office on Nashville's Music Row. Ten years later found me running six miles, four or five times a week along Belle Meade Blvd. or a four mile loop I'd devised, on the horse trails in Percy Warner Park. Eventually, I preferred the horse trails and ceased running on the street altogether. What an incredible rush, running by myself in the heat up in the woods. Flat out, up and down hills for around forty minutes. Sometimes, when I'd exit the woods and hit the pavement on the loop back to the front entrance, I'd feel so good I'd keep just running for another ten or fifteen minutes, never wanting to stop.

Occasionally, I'd see something strange in the woods. Once I encountered a large snake of some sort with the back half of a squirrel hanging out of its mouth. Sometimes I'd see a rattlesnake, and there were always the large paw prints of coyotes in the ditches by the side of the pavement as I walked up the hill, warming up before I hit the woods. And there were invariably deer, and an occasional bobcat.

A friend of mine with whom I'd frequently run or bike in the woods, had actually been attacked by an owl, of all things. It had simply swooped down on his head out of nowhere, and locked its talons into his hair and scalp, with the intention of snatching him up for dinner. He should have gone to see a doctor, but didn't, and consequently got some sort of dangerous infection as a result. After that, I became aware of the owls that would occasionally follow me as I ran. I'd seen one from time to time, but never more than one at a time, and it would usually be late afternoon or early evening. I'd never thought about them one way or the other until my friend had been selected for dinner.

Now, if an owl followed me, I realized that he was picking an opportune time and place to attempt to snatch me up off of the trail for his evening meal. To hell with that! Now, if I noticed an owl, I'd stop my watch, pick up a few rocks, and start sending them in its direction along with a kindly expressed warning such as 'Beat it you son of a bitch!' After that, he'd fly away, and that was that.

One evening, I saw on the nightly Nashville news that a man had been running down West End Avenue, across the street from Montgomery Bell Academy and had been attacked by an owl. The reporter did not mention the victim's name, and I thought no more about the incident, until twenty years later when I picked up a friend for lunch one Saturday. Since he, like myself, was a runner, I casually mentioned that a friend of mine had been attacked by an owl in Percy Warner Park, and that I'd seen on the news that an owl had plopped down on some hapless runner in this very neighborhood about twenty years ago.

"That was me," he said.

I laughed

"It was strange," he said. "On a day like today, nice, bright, without a cloud in the sky, I walked to the end of my driveway and started running, as usual. I hadn't gone far, when suddenly something smacked the back of my head. I immediately stopped and looked around in every direction, but there was no sign of anything out of the ordinary. I thought that perhaps it was my imagination, and resumed running. I hadn't gone much further and it happened again. This time, I knew it wasn't my imagination. I stopped and looked around again, and saw nothing. At this point, I determined that it was probably, or at least, could be a ghost."

"A ghost?" I laughed again, this time at my friend's default theory, that since he didn't know what it was, his attacker was most likely an agent of the supernatural. That my friend, a physician, and a man of science, had immediately reached this conclusion was humorous to say the least.

"The third time it happened, I saw the flash of a wing of some sort, and looking around, noticed an owl on one of the trees nearby."

"But this happened during daylight, right?"

"Yes, but an owl also got me on West End at night."

"The same one?"

"I don't know."

"That type of aggressive behavior from birds directed specifically toward members of the human species seldom occurs in the absence of some sort of blatant provocation," I observed jokingly. "What had you done?"

"Nothing. I was just minding my own business."

"Filthy avian bastard!" I replied. "You have to watch them." One night I was awakened from a deep sleep by one of the 'fowl-mouthed' creatures. It wouldn't shut up. I knew immediately what to do. I looked out the bathroom window and saw the big son of a bitch perched on the branch of a tree, just sitting there hooting loudly, silhouetted by the moonlight. He was nearly two feet tall. I got a bottle rocket, stuck it in the barrel of a pistol, opened the back door, lit the fuse, and off it went in the direction of the owl. It was a perfect shot and was heading straight toward him. As it was about to strike him dead center, the owl, maintaining both his composure, and his position, simply tilted sharply to the left as it passed, deftly avoiding the rocket, none the worse for the experience. When the rocket exploded, the owl took off."

"Yeah, you've got to keep an eye on them."

44. "THAT ISN'T MINE ! ! !"

She carefully packed the cosmetics case, which along with her small suitcase and purse, would accompany her on a weekend trip to meet her boyfriend in Atlanta. She was running late this Friday afternoon and would have to really move it if she wanted to make it to the Nashville Airport in Friday evening rush hour traffic, find a place in short term parking, and reach her plane in time.

She raced through the terminal with her cosmetics case in one hand, her carry-on bag over her shoulder, and her purse in her other hand, finally reaching the security scanner with mere moments to spare as she could hear the call for final boarding of her flight in the distance. She quickly placed her two bags and purse on the scanner's conveyor belt, emptied her pockets and stepped through the tall security scanner without incident, intent on grabbing her bags at the other end and sprinting the remaining distance to her departure gate.

"Step over here, please, and open that case. There appears to be something in it and I need to see what it is," the security guard said, stepping around the conveyor belt as the scanner buzzed loudly.

"What now?!" she asked loudly, angrily expressing her disapproval as she fumbled through her purse searching for the small key which would unlock her case.

"Open it," the security officer instructed coldly, now eyeing her suspiciously.

She opened the case and said, "There you go. Have fun."

To her surprise, there was a bath towel folded inside the case which the officer removed and unfolded. 'What was going on?' she wondered. She'd never seen this towel before, and it wasn't there when she'd locked her case before leaving for the airport. Her mind scanned her memory rapidly, seeking an explanation, but no, she was certain she'd never seen it before. The mystery of the inexplicable presence of the towel was heightened as the security officer unfolded it revealing a large anatomically correct, flesh colored dildo with a metal crank extending from its base. It was the metal crank which had obviously set off the alarm.

"That's not mine," she said quickly. "I've never seen it before."

"You'll have to leave that here mam," the officer said with a smirk, as he closed her case, "but you are free to go. Have fun!" he shouted after as she fled toward the gate, leaving 'it' in plain view on the counter.

Meanwhile, back at work, Dave stepped into my office, looked at his watch, and remarked with a laugh that it was 5:30, and by now Linda was probably in the plane and on her way to Atlanta.

"And?" I asked, looking up from my desk.

He proceeded to explain how he'd picked the lock on her American Tourister travel case and wrapped 'The Home Wrecker' as it was called, inside a towel, placed it in her case, and then locked the case again. "Boy, she's going to get a surprise."

And indeed she did. I laughed about it all weekend.

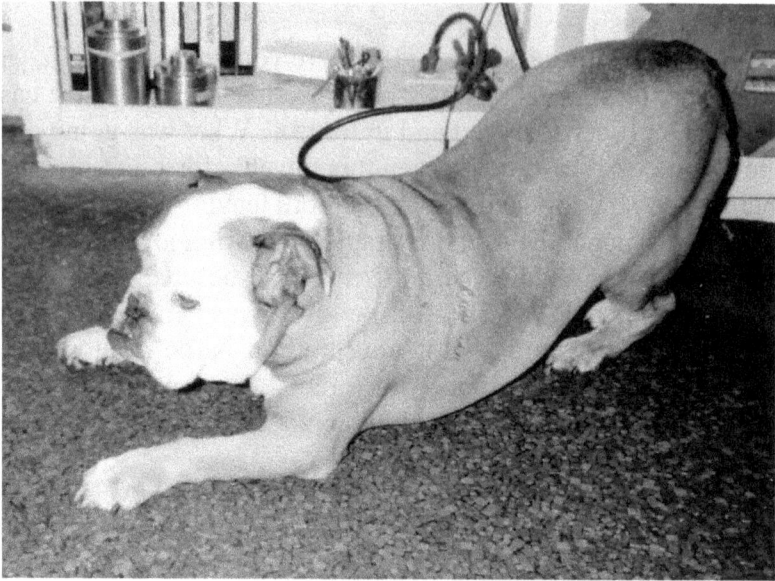

Perhaps he should learn to toot the clarinet.

45. EXPRESS YOURSELF

Any fan of Tennessee Williams knows that he had English Bulldogs, and how stupid and nasty they were, or are, if you happen to have one at present. My Mom brought me one when I was two years old. I still remember the cute little puppy in the big cardboard box. Out of all the subsequent ones I owned between then and now, she was the only bulldog that had any sense at all.

By the time I was in my 20s I'd moved on to German shepherds, which were very intelligent and intuitive. I had two, both of which were rescues. One day my Mom called from Arizona and said that there was an English Bulldog in the local paper that the owners were giving away. A two year old brindle female. She offered to bring her to me. Sure, why not?

In the last decade, I'd forgotten how stupid they really are. When my parents returned to town, I drove out to get the dog. It wasn't especially responsive to external stimuli, which should have been a warning sign. I also noticed that the creature upon our first meeting stood there motionless, like a cow for about 45 minutes. Perhaps she wasn't that smart. Well, at least she could keep my shepherds company while I was at work all day.

The dog stretched out on the back seat of my Cadillac convertible, for the ride home, basking in the sunlight like a sack of feed. I soon realized that she was having trouble breathing. Basically she was inhaling the flaps of her own nose with every breath when she was hot, forcing her to breathe through her mouth. If she was to be a regular passenger in my car with the top down, this would have to be dealt with. I took her to the vet, who said that she needed a nose job. "I don't believe that cosmetic surgery will improve her appearance," I opined, "but if it enables her to ride in the car with the top down, go ahead." Privately, I wondered what was next. Multiple breast augmentation? The nose job fixed the problem with riding in the car. It did not, however, improve her personality. Sometimes, when we'd reach our destination, I'd try to get her to jump out of the car, without incident. Often, she'd refuse to move. After about ten seconds of non-compliance, I'd grab her by the collar and drag her out, at which time she'd bite me rapidly, and I'd bitch slap her back and forth with my open hand, cursing her loudly. It was sort of like having a girlfriend that you don't particularly like, but are too busy to actually get around to breaking up with, knowing in the back of your mind that in truth, she doesn't especially like you either.

Tandy, as I'd named her did not like rain, and rather than going into the garage or under the back porch when it rained, would stand rigidly on all four legs looking angrily at the sky and barking loudly as the rain pounded her. She constantly started fights with the female German shepherd, contests which she invariably lost. It usually started like this: I'd be sitting quietly in my den, reading a book and smoking a cigar, and I'd look up and see the bulldog standing there motionless, just staring at the sleeping shepherd who was minding her own business. The shepherd always tried to avoid the icy basilisk stare of the bulldog, but would invariably look up from time to time to see if the bulldog was still staring at her. This eye contact, however brief, further enflamed the ire of the bulldog, whose sides would begin moving in and out rapidly as her body became more and more rigid. At this point, any sudden movement or loud noise on my part would cause the bulldog to lunge at the shepherd. Finding this interaction between them both amusing and humorous, I'd suddenly stomp my foot loudly, or quietly close my book and then slam it loudly against the floor without advance notice. As soon as the loud noise was made, the bulldog jumped the shepherd. The shepherd would then get atop the bulldog and grab her by the loose skin on the top of her neck and go to work, always winning the confrontation. It was almost a nightly ritual, and always ended the same way. The bulldog started the fight and the shepherd ended it, a further confirmation of the bulldog's stupidity.

The bulldog was not only stupid, but lazy. I took her for one or two 'walks' around the neighborhood, nothing long or arduous, just a walk. When the bulldog decided the walk was over, that was it. She'd simply sit down without notice and wouldn't move any further. I'd have to pick her up, throw her over my shoulder, and lug her back home.

To say the dog was nasty would be a grave understatement. She would drop a log in the house without warning if the need arose, rather than express any desire to take it outdoors. Armed with that knowledge, I generally left the dog outside while I was at work. One day, it had been cold, so in consideration of the dog's sensitive feelings, I left it inside the house. I returned from work to the sound of my fire alarm. I hurried into the house, looking for smoke. As soon as I opened the door, I discovered what had set off the smoke alarm. The dog had taken a crap that was so foul, and stunk so badly, that the heavily laden particulate essence actually set off the smoke alarm.

On nice days, I'd take her to work and she'd more or less behave, sleeping all day wherever she pleased, her tongue hanging out of her mouth, its end dry and stretched out on the floor beyond her fleshy, prognathic jaws. I'd walk by upon occasion as she snored and silently grab the dry end of her tongue between my thumb and forefinger and give it a quick shake and then let it go before she had time to react and bite me. I'd do this at home too, so much, that she'd open one eye when anyone passed by. Her face would still be spread out across the floor, motionless, and she'd still have her dry tongue hanging out, and she'd still be snoring, but that one eye would move around like a searchlight.

One day, one of my employees thought he might nudge her with his shoe while she was asleep. The dog went from fast asleep and stretched out on the floor snoring, to having its jaws instantly locked on my friend's ankle, fully demonstrating her incredible speed from zero to sixty in less than two seconds.

Like Tennessee Williams' bulldog, mine simply walked away from the office one day. It had been a nice spring morning outside and the women had propped the front door open. When it was quitting time, I began looking for the dog and couldn't find her. She must have just wandered off. I certainly wasn't prepared to waste time driving around town hollering out the window looking for the stupid creature. I should have taken advantage of the opportunity I'd been afforded, but instead, made the same mistake as Tennessee Williams had. I placed an ad in the paper offering a reward for its return. After a few days I received a phone call and described my dog to the caller, and the circumstances under which she'd disappeared. He didn't want a reward but said that he'd taken the dog to his vet and had it checked out and given appropriate shots and would like to be reimbursed. He said the dog had been found several blocks away from my office, and appeared lost. Apparently the dumb son of a bitch had walked from Music Row down to West End and to Wendy's, where she'd been rescued from the incredible traffic as she followed someone who was carrying a big sack of hamburgers.

With mounting regret I drove to pick up the dog. I should have let him keep the dog and told him that no, she wasn't mine after all. I could have been rid of her once and for all. None of my girlfriends liked the filthy thing, and as I mentioned, neither did I, really. It ended up costing me more than $350 to get her back. I walked out to the garage in back of the house one morning to get a car and go to work. As usual, the dog was asleep in the driveway and I greeted her sarcastically, as always, "Thanks so much for guarding the house so diligently while I slept last night." I slowly backed the car out of the garage and got out of it to move her out of the way, like I did every morning. She'd once had her leg run over by a friend, because she was too lazy or stupid to get out of the way of his car. So it was a real consideration. This time, she didn't move, despite my

119

cursing. She had gone to glory as they say in these parts, to her eternal reward. I lamented her passage for a couple of minutes, lowered the top, and was on my way, resolved to be done forever with bulldogs.

I had several years of peace, and then one day I received a call from a friend who had an extra English bulldog that she didn't need. She asked if I'd want him. It was a nice spring morning, I was in a good mood, so I said yes, and went to get him. He was white and tan and was more energetic and `intelligent' if I may use that word, than his predecessor. We got along well and he had a good personality. We played out in the yard and in the house and had a really good time. I was pleased with him and happy to have him.

He was nasty, as all English bulldogs are, and stank equally from both ends, coming or going. He eventually developed an odious and strange habit of literally grinding his ass on the corner edge of one of the porch steps leading up to the back door. He would regularly engage in this puzzling activity, grinding away, amidst loudly vocalized expressions of either agony or ecstasy, I wasn't sure which. He'd accompany these activities with quaint facial expressions as he threw his body into it, grinding, howling, and shaking his head. Personally, I didn't care if he ground the corner of the step to a nub. It was nothing to me. At length, however, I began to think that perhaps I should take him to New Orleans, put him in front of the St. Louis Cathedral with a sombrero on his head, and let him put on a show for the tourists. I could put a tip jar and a ghetto blaster next to him, give him a brick to grind his ass on, and just collect money while he did his thing.

Instead, I took him to the vet down the street. Maybe there was something wrong with him, apart from the obvious. He was taken into an examination room while I waited in the lobby. After a few minutes, I was summoned, and the vet told me that `Coochie' needed to `express himself.' I replied that the dog was free to express himself in any manner he deemed desirable.

"It's fine with me," I told her. "He can howl at the moon if he likes, it doesn't matter to me one way or the other."

She explained that I might perhaps have misunderstood her, so she again stated that Coochie needed to express himself. I assumed he could take up painting, learn to play the piano, or something else, and said as much.

"No," she replied, "he needs to express his anal glands."

"Nobody's stopping him."

"You are going to need to insert your finger inside his anus a couple of times a week and push around the edges to release…"

I cut her off quickly. "I don't foresee that happening…ever. That is definitely not going to happen."

"Well," she continued, "he's going to continue rubbing on the back porch stairs as you've described unless you do that. He's had his glands expressed today so it won't be necessary to repeat the process for several days."

"I see why you get the big money," I said.

She wasn't amused. Obviously she considered me remiss in the care of my pet, and insensitive as well.

I'm happy to report that the dog lived to be 14 years old, making him the most elderly bulldog I'd ever personally known. I attribute his longevity to a constant diet of Krystal hamburgers, Mexican food, donuts, an occasional beer, and entire chocolate pies. He never took up a musical instrument, but did continue to grind away upon that particular back porch step, with what I deemed considerable pleasure and enthusiasm.

46. THE GIFT OF THE DOUBLE REVERSE MAGI

It was a match made in heaven, well, not really. At least it was a love match. Well, it wasn't really that either. She was just horny, that's all. She already had three juvenile delinquent brats from her former husband. "I was going to have sex with somebody that night, I didn't care who," she told the groom's mother several weeks before the wedding, a shotgun affair, in the figurative and literal sense of the word, after she'd turned up pregnant. As my yardman observed, 'a hard dick has no conscience, or judgment,' or as an older lady once told me, 'when women chase men, men don't know how to run.'

So the woman had turned up pregnant. Surprise, surprise. Perhaps she was pregnant already, who knows? Anyway, when her father found out about her situation he saw an opportunity to unload the entire brood on an intelligent and successful although not particularly streetwise, dupe. He couldn't feign outrage that his daughter had been misused. It was years too late for that. What he could do, however was make a deal with the new pigeon in which the latter would actually adopt the other three minor children, in which case, the financial anchor and chain he'd been lugging for years would be removed, a pleasant thought to be sure.

To that end, he met with the soon to be groom, and prevailed upon his delicate and paternal sensibilities. "Look, these children need a father, not just a father figure. Here's what I'm willing to do. I'll send you on an all expense paid honeymoon, anywhere you like. I'll continue to pay all of their medical insurance, so they won't be any sort of financial burden on you. I've been lucky in life, so I have enough money to make things run smoothly for you. Furthermore, I'll pay off the mortgage on that house she lives in, and buy you some land. You will, of course, need to formally, that is, legally adopt the children."

Although the groom had been making plenty of money, he didn't happen to have any at just the moment, despite some recent high profile work for major international companies. His expenses frequently exceeded what he charged for any project and his work was seldom completed on time. In other words, his employees were doing fine, but he never actually 'made any money.' This looked like a good deal for him, since the old man was rich and willing to foot the bill.

The future bride didn't know any of this back room dealing was going on between her father and the pigeon. She didn't know that the groom didn't have any money. In fact, she was glad he happened to be the person she latched onto this time since he was clearly rich, at least as far as she knew. His family was prosperous and lived in one of the best neighborhoods in the closest city, about forty miles away. They also owned a three bedroom condo overlooking the beach in south Florida. Her intended had a nice car, a wonderful custom built shop with an attached residence. He had expensive clothes several expensive motorcycles, one of which he kept in Germany which he used when skiing in the Swiss Alps. This was indeed her lucky day. Now she would never have to work again.

The groom was equally pleased if not especially jubilant, since the bride's father was rich and had promised him much.

He figured the old man was good for the long run, and that he would be so appreciative of seeing her in a happy place, that he'd be glad to pay the freight, whatever it might ultimately prove to be.

The groom's family however, were understandably much less jubilant and suggested a 'paternity test.' If their son wasn't the father of the forthcoming bundle of joy, he might be less likely to 'do the right thing.' In light of the intended bride's past history, it seemed to be a logical precaution. The groom considered this to be an offensive suggestion as it potentially impugned the character of his er, uh, beloved.

And so the couple were wed, went on their sea cruise to Alaska, and the great northwest, as promised. After they returned from their so-called honeymoon, the old man was ready to get down to business. He wanted those children adopted legally, and out of his hair once and for all, as he'd made some poor investments recently, and was running out of money sooner rather than later. And of course, unbeknownst to the groom, the daughter really was violent and crazy, and capable of fits of rage reminiscent of a wounded Cape Buffalo. She'd smashed her former husband's car windshield with a baseball bat while he was in the car. She'd gone on rampages and kicked holes in the walls of her nice house. She refused to discipline her children and became loud and aggressive if anybody said anything which appeared to teach them anything remotely resembling proper public deportment.

Almost as soon as the groom signed the necessary papers to complete the adoption process, the flow of money ceased. The children's medical insurance payments stopped and the groom was left holding the bag, so to speak.

The groom did his best but soon realized his wife was nuts. Still, he attempted to be a good father even after he was finally able to get divorced, but his efforts were largely fruitless. His so-called son in a fit of rage reminiscent of his mother's, smashed the windshield of the groom's Alfa-Romeo roadster and bashed the hood and fenders with a sledge hammer. The other children frequently stole things from his shop, used his credit cards up without his knowledge or permission.

Most recently, his adopted daughter, the 'daughter from a

previous marriage' threatened to never speak to him again if he refused to pay for her third marriage, all the while knowing that he couldn't afford it. "You could sell the timber off of your land," she suggested remorselessly.

My grandmother told me at age nine, that I should never go to bed with any girl I didn't want to marry. I told her that I wouldn't. "Can I go fishing now?"

As my yard man once sagely observed, "The con man makes it off somebody who wants something for nothing. There's no such thing." The groom had been conned as easily as any hick at a county fair.

Giant crawdad. Near Jeanerette, Louisiana

47. NEXT !

"The secret is in the bread," she said as we stood there in line at this New Orleans French Quarter landmark. We came to the Crescent City often, before & after Hurricane Katrina, and always stopped at this quaint restaurant at least once for lunch, and then again for a sandwich to take with us on the trip home. It was actually an Italian grocery which had been in the same location and owned by the same family since the early 1900s, the sort of nondescript place you'd normally just walk past without noticing it if you weren't already familiar with it. But the sublime and pervasive aroma of olives, olive oil, garlic, and various cheeses that had seeped into the walls for decades was both unmistakable and irresistible. Occasionally as the front door opened, a passerby would get a whiff and stop and step inside to see what could possibly smell that wonderful.

The store was rectangular in shape, not especially large but festively arrayed shelves almost floor to ceiling on both walls with cans and bottles of olive oil, jars of various types of sauces, pickles, capers, and cheeses, teas, and coffees for sale, as well as large decorative jars of various sizes and shapes filled with colorful peppers soaking in olive oil. Two heavy black cast iron ceiling fans from early 20th Century buzzed and droned overhead, adding to the authentic Italian ambience of the place.

Although the store sold a variety of items, most patrons seldom bought anything other than the sandwiches known as muffelettas, which are sold as premade half or whole sizes only, and prewrapped in white butcher paper. New Orleans is every bit as famous for the muffeletta as it is for seafood gumbo, jambalaya, or crawfish etouffee. The whole sandwich is almost as big around as a good size apple pie and is more than enough to eat for two people. It consists of a particular kind of large round bread which is sliced horizontally to which is then applied on the lower half a sort of olive spread which is composed of finely chopped olives, celery, cauliflower, capers, and carrots bathed in olive oil. The olive oil seeps into the bread as the sandwich is assembled. Then several slices of various cheeses are applied over that including provolone, and Swiss. Next, on top of that, are very thinly sliced ham, salami, and other meats.

To the rear, at the very back of the store are two counters, one of which has one surface, the other has two, where patrons may eat. It is a self-service place in the strictest sense of the word. There were no waiters and nobody to help the customer with anything whatsoever, just a cashier.

There are different people 'on duty' from one day to the next, most of whom are in some way related to the owners of the place, whoever they may be. Most of the sandwiches are premade either the night before or in the morning prior to opening. It's said that the secret is in the bread, but whatever the secret, they are always fresh and delicious. The only employees any customer will have any interaction with are cashiers, usually one, but sometimes two. They aren't very friendly, generally speaking. There's one in particular who I've noticed during my many visits to the restaurant over the past 25 years that I've been actively visiting New Orleans. He has slicked back black hair, and is sort of stocky, thick, for lack of a better word. He's about 5'10" in height, adorned in polyester shirt and trousers and proudly wears his gold jewelry. He resembles one of the 'Sopranos' extras, and could just as easily be from New Jersey as New Orleans.

He never greets his customers warmly or with a smile, but then neither do any of the other cashiers. It's obvious that Sal, Jr. and his brothers, cousins, or whoever the hell the other cashiers might be, would rather be somewhere else, anywhere else. Over the years that I'd seen him there, I realized that he was an ass. In fact, everyone who worked there was a jerk. How hard can it be? You sell sandwiches somebody else has made and you get your cut of the family business. You don't really have any heavy responsibilities wearing you down, at least none associated with work, apart from the usual inter family jealousies which exist within a family business where the ownership has been diluted between sons, daughters, and in laws, and grandchildren, over a century or longer. Still, if your attitude is that bad, move aside and let someone else do the job.

I resolved to get my sandwiches somewhere else. After all, muffelettas were as common in New Orleans as cockroaches, rats, and drunken panhandlers. There were plenty of other options, and I took them, including The Court of Two Sisters, Antoine's annex, and Napoleon House. All of them had excellent muffelettas, and yet, despite my firm resolutions, I'd return to this particular place frequently. Each time I'd experience the usual rudeness, I'd renew my vows. But there I was one bright summer morning, and there was a long line already. I seldom wait in lines, anywhere, ever, but on this particular day I wasn't in a hurry and this is what I wanted for

126

lunch, so it didn't matter. As I got closer to the cashier, I realized that I was going to get Sal, Jr. again. He'd seen me literally dozens of times over the years by now, and should've recognized me on sight. He'd never acknowledged me, or even smiled, in all of this time, basically a quarter of a century. But, as I got closer, our eyes met, and for the first time. In that instant I got it that he actually hated his customers, the hundreds, no, the thousands of different and nameless faces he'd seen nearly every day of his life. He read in my eyes that I understood his situation, and his life. He smiled and so did I. The sandwiches were both his salvation and the chains which had bound him from birth.

I never disliked him after that, and he'd nod when he saw me. His life had been foreordained from birth. He would continue as part owner of the family business, and would make a good living doing so, but he'd never be really rich, or free. He'd never know the risks of stepping out on his own, the fear of failure, or the thrill of accomplishing something by himself.

THE ARGUMENT

It was just an argument, a difference of opinion. No, it wasn't an argument. Not really. Most arguments have some point, and this didn't. There was no advantage sought, no attempt at persuasion, and nothing to be gained on either side. This was spontaneous and vicious, without any lead in or advance notice. It just was. She accusingly demanded to know what I'd done with her new can of stain for the gate. I didn't know what she was talking about. We'd been to the paint store an hour ago and she'd bought four gallons of paint which I'd carried to the car and loaded, then unloaded when we'd returned home. I didn't know anything about any `stain.'

"The gallon can of stain I bought at the store?!!!" she again demanded angrily. I reacted with equal hostility to her implication that I'd lost, mishandled, or in some other way was responsible for her can of whatever. I still didn't know what she was talking about, but I answered her in the same manner in which I'd been asked, shouting. "There's a can of paint on the back seat floor, behind me! Is that it?" I yelled at this person who I love more than anybody or anything on earth. "You can't talk to me like that!" I shouted angrily.

Suddenly, it was my fault that she'd picked a fight. To hear her tell it, she'd merely asked me nicely if I'd seen her can of stain. She hadn't shouted, she told me, she'd actually asked me in a nice, pleasant voice. But I know what I'd heard. She'd talked to me like a dog, over nothing, treating me like one of her friends treats her husband. She seems to think I'm him, that I have to take that kind of abuse. I don't have to, and I won't.

In full auto defense mode, I was already weighing my options. I have a house in Mississippi, I've got money. I'm debt free. A small moving van could get my stuff out of her house in less than an hour, and a car hauler could get my cars to Mississippi with a day's notice. I'd be none the worse for this or any other experience. I'm not married and have the freedom to do whatever I want, whenever I want. The freedom to stay or the freedom to go. I'd left women I'd really loved before because I'd been taken for granted. The truth of the matter is that in all my relationships with all of the women I've ever known, she is the only one I've never cheated on. Sometimes I feel like a ten round fighter in the middle of a twenty-six round fight. I can do better!

But angry words spoken thoughtlessly over something that doesn't matter, do very much matter, and an apology doesn't remove the damage done. The apology is accepted and life goes on, but the damage is cumulative. It is done and filed away, even if unconsciously, and over time, one simply ceases to `see' the person they love so much. And then one day, she, who was your best friend for the better part of your life, doesn't, matter anymore, and you no longer matter to her. The years of innumerable kindness, laughter, and shared joy are dismissed, as casually as if they'd never happened.

Meanwhile, outside, the cicadas were buzzing, the birds singing, and the warm breeze blowing through the car windows as we each shouted angry accusations back and forth on this summer evening, oblivious to its beauty, and to the unearned and very fleeting gifts that we've both been given.

Even as she continued blaming and berating me, I was as guilty of this `argument' over nothing as she was. I could have ignored her accusatory tone and just listened to what she was trying to say beneath the hostility. And I'm frequently as guilty or worse myself, of being unpleasant, sarcastic, and accusatory, generally without reason or justification. I also knew that despite my anger at that moment, she is the love of my heart, and the reason I've chosen her above everyone else, is because I've never met anyone like her. She is truly the kindest, most beautiful soul I've ever known, and the greatest gift I've ever received. That is who she is.

Even so, I will leave her one day, and sooner rather than later, or she will leave me. It's easy enough to do the math. We have more time together behind us now than ahead, and one of us, whoever is left, will remember this day at some point with deep regret and a sincere, but impossible wish to relive even one of the countless joy filled, carefree days we've spent together. But it will be too late then.

Since I don't know when that last day will arrive, it is important for me to remember that right now, this very moment, is all I really have, and it is literally passing from me, slipping away, even as I'm too ungrateful, arrogant, self-important, or just preoccupied, to recognize it for the gift it truly is.

SMOKE 'EM IF YOU GOT 'EM

In the late 1960s, before lifetime government politicians sought to legislate and or tax every human activity in an effort to prolong their time at the taxpayer trough, one could smoke pretty much anywhere. There were intelligent exceptions of course, such as in the immediate proximity of a gasoline tanker unloading fuel, or inside a dynamite factory.

The military was especially lenient regarding tobacco use during the Viet Nam era, and would dubiously reward its servicemen throughout the day with welcome words such as 'Smoke 'em if you got 'em,' or 'the smoking lamp is lit,' both of which were spoken at the discretion of whoever was in charge. His power to make these pronouncements was confirmed by the ever present symbols of his authority, a cigarette and a coffee mug, and the ability to wield them simultaneously with fearless impunity, even in the presence of those further up the chain of command.

I didn't especially care for cigarettes at this time and smoked cigars. Anyway, at Advanced Undersea Weapons School in Key

West, we were permitted to smoke in class. I wasn't particularly fond of the instructor on general principles, not that he'd done anything specifically which irritated me beyond mispronouncing his own name. Monet is correctly pronounced 'Mo-nay', not 'Mo-Net,' which might have, in some circles, been improperly if understandably misconstrued as a slang basketball term. What I perhaps disliked most about him was the arrogance of his ignorance, which at the time exceeded even my own. He'd correctly pronounced and used the word 'adhere' in one of his rambling, sleep-inducing lectures. Since that was a big word for him, he emphasized it for us morons by taking a piece of chalk and writing 'ADHEAR !' on the blackboard in foot tall letters. There was no point in correcting him in front of the class on either his blatant misspelling, or the inability to properly pronounce his own name. So the days drudged on, and he indeed proved himself to be a knowledgeable instructor even though I didn't particularly like him, or he, me.

One day we were not seated as usual, but were standing around looking at some mines, torpedoes, and other undersea ordnance. They were all real, but had been disarmed. As we stood gathered around each, one at a time, Monet would use a pointer to show the various parts of each weapon and describe its operation and function. Some of them were rather large, exceeding five or six feet in length, and all were mounted atop moveable stands, each of which were at approximately waste level. There was one device in particular which was very large and long, with a lengthwise opening which ran unobstructed from one end through its middle, and out the other end. I correctly surmised that this torpedo would be Monet's next stop, so I blew several mouthfuls of cigar smoke through the stern opening of the weapon and then waited. Sure enough, he moved to the torpedo and with his pointer, began lecturing, and tapping on its nose. Suddenly, he became silent and immobile, instantly transfixed, his face turning a deathly white at the sight of smoke emanating from the torpedo's front end where its explosives are housed. At that moment I started laughing like a hyena, which broke the spell. "Faragher!" he immediately shouted, "five laps around the football field! Now! Move it!" At first I could barely run for laughing so hard, but five laps in the midday heat calmed me down to the degree that I was at length able to reenter class without laughing out loud, but it had been worth it. `Smoke `em if you got `em, Mo-Net!'

www.ingramcontent.com/pod-product-compliance
Lightning Source LLC
Chambersburg PA
CBHW070808280326
41934CB00012B/3106